Working Ethics

of related interest

Working Relationships
Spirituality in Human Service and Organisational Life
Neil Pembroke
ISBN 1 84310 252 8

Community Care Practice and the Law
Third Edition
Michael Mandelstam
ISBN 1 84310 233 1

In Living Color
An Intercultural Approach to Pastoral Care and Counseling
Second Edition
Emmanuel Y. Lartey
Foreword by James Newton Poling
ISBN 1 84310 750 3

Social Work, Immigration and Asylum
Debates, Dilemmas and Ethical Issues for Social Work and Social Care
Practice
Edited by Debra Hayes and Beth Humphries
Foreword by Steve Cohen
ISBN 1 84310 194 7

Law, Rights and Disability
Edited by Jeremy Cooper
ISBN 1 85302 836 3

Ethical Practice and the Abuse of Power in Social Responsibility
Leave No Stone Unturned
Edited by Helen Payne and Brian Littlechild
ISBN 1 85302 743 X

Cultural Competence in the Caring Professions
Kieran O'Hagan
ISBN 1 85302 759 6

Working Ethics

How to be Fair in a Culturally Complex World

Richard Rowson

Jessica Kingsley Publishers
London and Philadelphia

First published in 2006
by Jessica Kingsley Publishers
116 Pentonville Road
London N1 9JB, UK
and
400 Market Street, Suite 400
Philadelphia, PA 19106, USA

www.jkp.com

Library of Congress Cataloging in Publication Data
A CIP catalog record for this book is available from the Library of Congress

British Library Cataloguing in Publication Data
Rowson, Richard.
Working ethics : how to be fair in a culturally complex world / Richard Rowson.-- 1st American ed.
p. cm.
Includes bibliographical references and index.
ISBN-13: 978-1-85302-750-5 (pbk.)
ISBN-10: 1-85302-750-2 (pbk.)
1. Professional ethics. I. Title.
BJ1725.R69 2006
174--dc22

2005034523

ISBN 10: 1 85302 750 2
ISBN 13: 978 1 85302 750 5

Printed and bound in Great Britain by
Athenaeum Press, Gateshead, Tyne and Wear

To Julian

Contents

Acknowledgements

I thank Julian Mitchell and Christopher Robbins for reading drafts of this book and for their encouraging and constructive suggestions. I also thank Julian for his unfailing support during its writing.

I am very grateful to Annabel Jones for putting me in touch with Jessica Kingsley, and to Jessica for being prepared to publish a book with such a wide sweep of ideas.

My grateful thanks to Bridgit Dimond and Verena Tschudin for their advice, and my thanks to everyone at Jessica Kingsley Publishers.

Introduction

For over 2000 years philosophers, religious leaders and others have argued about how people should behave, what morality is, and what is the true or correct source of ethical guidance. In the cultural complexity of modern societies people in professions are often uncertain what guidance to follow. This book puts forward an ethical foundation for them. Its aim is to encourage members of professions to reflect on the values they espouse in their practice and, if they agree with the view put forward, to give them confidence in values that are appropriate for their work in culturally complex democratic societies.

The term 'professions' is used in this book to mean organisations and associations whose members deploy their expertise and powers to promote objectives that are valuable for the individuals who recieve their services and for the societies in which they operate. These objectives include health and social care (health and social care professions), justice and the protection of the law (legal professions and the police), safe communities (the police), safe and well-designed built environments (architects, engineers), financial probity (accountancy), equitable social policies and administration (civil servants) and learning (education).

This book shows that certain values are necessary for professionals working in all sections of the community to fulfil their role successfully. Those professionals – for example, some priests, rabbis and imams – who see their remit as limited to certain groups in society, and whose work is imbued with particular cultural or religious values, may find that parts of the book do not apply to their work.

The book puts forward an ethical framework that has four basic values, which may be summarised by the useful mnemonic 'FAIR':

1. Fairness

2. respect for Autonomy

3. Integrity

4. seeking the most beneficial and least harmful consequences, or **R**esults.

These values can enable professionals to:

- work effectively within culturally complex democracies

- earn the trust of people using their services

- be mutually supportive of the work of other professions

- promote democratic ideals

- be fair in their treatment of people of different cultures.

By looking at situations likely to occur in different professions the book shows how these values can provide ethical guidelines. It suggests ways in which the values may be interpreted and related to practice by professionals working on their own or as members of professional and advisory bodies. Note that these ways are suggestions only, they do not prescribe what individuals should do in actual situations. Examples are put forward simply to illustrate points in the text, not to recommend ways of acting in particular circumstances. Given the complexity of situations, and the number of factors professionals must take into account when judging the appropriate action to take, it would be improper for a book to try to do this. The responsibility for deciding what to do in particular situations must remain with the professionals concerned.

The book provides a sweep of ideas for professionals to consider, and there are questions at the end of each chapter to encourage them to do this. It does not provide information about the statutory and legal obligations of professionals, nor about the professional guidelines, codes of conduct or regulatory procedures issued by professions, professional bodies and other relevant organisations. Members of all professions should ensure they are familiar with the current legal and professional requirements and should give them precedence over suggestions presented here. This book gives a framework for making ethical decisions in the many situations where such requirements do *not* prescribe what professionals should do.

Part One identifies fundamental values integral to fulfilling the role of professions in culturally complex democracies. Part Two looks at the obligations that may arise from adherence to these values expressed as principles; exploration of the issues that can occur forms the core of this part. Part Three begins by considering how the values may be incorporated within professional practice, and finishes with considerations of blame and rights.

Chapter 11, on blame, argues for limits to the extent to which professionals can be held to be blameworthy. It offers an approach to debriefing procedures that, while enabling lessons to be learned, tries to avoid individuals being unjustly blamed. The chapter on rights explains different forms of rights and shows how the values put forward in the book can help resolve conflicts between them.

Readers wishing to consider other views on ethics in the professions, or in exploring the many cultural, religious and ethical views that people hold, should refer to the books in the Further Reading section at the end of the book.

A note on the use of words in this book

In this book, as in normal usage, the terms 'ethics' and 'morality' are used interchangeably to refer to general ideas about right and wrong, good and bad. 'Ethics' is *not* used here to mean 'the formal study of morality', as when students take a course in 'ethics'.

If ever it is necessary to refer to the formal rules, codes of conduct or conventionally accepted ways of behaving in a particular profession, these will be identified by reference to the profession – for example, 'medical ethics', 'business ethics' or the 'ethics of the legal professions'.

The adjectives 'moral' and 'ethical' are used simply to mean 'relevant to morality and ethics', as in: 'I don't think the length of a man's hair is a moral/ethical matter.' So in the book 'ethical decision' means a decision that takes into account ethical considerations, not a decision that is necessarily ethically right or appropriate.

Reading this book

If you are not used to reading books on ethics you may find it difficult to read this book at your normal speed. As author I have done my best to explain the ideas as clearly as possible. Nonetheless, there may be places where you need to read a sentence more than once. If this is so, please accept my apologies. Castigate the author, not yourself.

Seeking Ethical Values for the Professions

In Part One we look at various sources of guidance on how we should behave and consider whether any of them can be shown to be the one true basis of ethics. After concluding that none can, we ask what ethical values members of professions should adopt. We answer this by reflecting on the role of professionals who work with people in all sections of culturally complex democracies. We see that certain values are necessary for them to fulfil this role successfully. In Part Two we will explore the obligations these values give to professionals, and in Part Three we will see how the values can provide a framework of principles to guide their practice.

Chapter 1

Sources of Guidance and the Basis of Ethics

Different sources

We generally see ethics as giving us a standpoint from which to decide what is right and wrong and what we ought or ought not to do. Ethics is not, however, the only source of guidance from which we judge behaviour to be acceptable and unacceptable. Every day we make such judgements from the perspectives of law, social convention, professional codes of conduct, religious beliefs, aesthetic taste, politics and practicality. Moreover we often consider a situation from the standpoints of more than one of these, as the following scenario demonstrates.

> A police patrol stops a car for exceeding the speed limit. The driver is a father desperate to get his heavily bleeding child to hospital. Although the police officers are aware that what the father did was *legally* wrong, they think it is *morally* right to try to save a life and so they help him reach the hospital by driving ahead of him with lights and sirens going.

Here follow some definitions and scenarios that make clear the different standpoints we use when making judgements about what is right and wrong.

Law

We judge behaviour as right or wrong from the legal standpoint when we consider whether it complies with, or goes against, the laws of a particular country.

Bull fighting is legal in Spain but illegal in the United Kingdom. Some people, however, think it is wrong to cause animals to suffer and so regard bull fighting as ethically unacceptable no matter where it takes place.

Social convention

We judge behaviour from the point of view of social convention or etiquette when we consider whether it is the accepted way of behaving in a particular community.

It is good etiquette in some communities for women to keep their heads covered in the presence of men; in other communities men are expected to open doors for women. Some people regard these customs as ethically objectionable because they think they encourage the idea that women are inferior to, or less capable than, men. Others, however, see these customs as ways by which members of one gender show respect for members of the other, so they regard them as ethically acceptable.

Professional codes of conduct

Codes of conduct set out procedures to be followed by members of an organisation or profession. Within a profession, behaviour is considered 'right' if it conforms to the relevant code.

For example, the United Kingdom Code of Conduct for National Health Service Managers (October 2002) says that managers should 'seek to ensure that:

- NHS resources are protected from fraud and corruption and that any incident of this kind is reported to the NHS Counter Fraud Services' (p.9)

It would be considered right for a manager to report such an incident, and wrong if she deliberately failed to do so.

Religious beliefs

In most religious traditions human behaviour is judged right or wrong according to how well it fits into an overall divine scheme.

In many religions the deity is seen as the giver and taker of life. To many believers it is therefore wrong for one person to kill another. However, throughout history many people, some religious believers and some not, have thought it *ethically* acceptable to take life in certain circumstances – for example, to punish murderers or to kill an enemy soldier in battle.

Visual and aesthetic sense

We often judge objects and actions acceptable and unacceptable by how well they accord with our own visual taste and artistic sensitivities.

A social worker has managed to get a client rehoused in better accommodation. When the client enthusiastically shows her how he has redecorated his room, the clashing colours and patterns offend her aesthetic sense. However, she thinks it ethically important to promote his self-esteem and so praises him for what he has achieved.

Practicality

From a practical standpoint we judge an act 'right' if it is the best way to achieve a particular objective.

We may decide that the right way to hang a picture on a concrete wall is to use a drill, plastic plug and screw, rather than a hammer and nail. The hammer and nail method may chip the wall, the nail lose its grip and the picture fall down. We may see the drill method as right from a practical standpoint and not see any other evaluative standpoint as relevant – law, ethics and social convention, for example, do not have anything to say about it.

Politics

We judge actions and policies from a political standpoint when we consider whether they will promote or hinder our political objectives.

Someone may think gambling is ethically unacceptable but consider it would be politically wrong of a government to ban it, as it would then lose the support of a large section of the population and so put at risk its chances of being re-elected.

Ethics

What constitutes the ethical standpoint is the subject of the rest of this chapter and the next. In the above scenarios ethics has been seen as quite separate from the other evaluative standpoints. Some people, however, question whether there really is a clear distinction between ethics and law and ethics and religion. The following sections consider different views on these relationships.

Views on the relationship between ethics and law[1]

There are various views on the relationship between ethics and law. One is that law and ethics are one and the same or, at least, inextricably entwined. Law is seen as a device for enforcing the ethical views of a society: so as long as we act within the law we act in ways that are ethically acceptable in our society. One objection to this view is that in societies in which there are several cultures there is insufficient agreement on ethical issues for the law to enforce anything that can be seen as an ethical consensus. Another objection is that the law permits behaviour that many people consider ethically unacceptable – gambling, high-pressure selling and arms dealing, for instance – so, for these people at least, ethics and law are distinct.

Many people think that not only does the law not enact ethics, but it would be wrong for it to do so. In their view, the law should allow individuals as much freedom as possible, and if it did not allow people the freedom to act in ways that some may regard as unethical it would be too restrictive – if, for example, the law were to declare telling lies illegal.

Moreover, many people consider the law too blunt an instrument to make the subtle judgements appropriate in ethics; imagine the difficulties of using the law to establish when it is and is not acceptable to tell a 'white lie'. Considerations such as these lead most people to regard law and ethics as different evaluative standpoints even though they may often see their demands as coinciding.

If we regard ethics as a separate source of guidance from law, what is the basis of ethics? We know where to find the basis of British law, for example – Parliament approves legislation to which the people are subject, or judges make judgements which become legal precedents – but what is the basis of ethics? What is its source?

A traditional answer to such questions is 'religion'.

Views on the relationship between ethics and religion

As with the relationship between ethics and law, there are different views on the relationship between ethics and religion.

Religious believers who make judgements about what is right and wrong solely on the basis of their religious beliefs see the two as indistinguishable. So some Christians see the wrongness of divorce as consisting in its offence against God's law, and some Muslims see the wrongness of taking life in certain circumstances as consisting in its contravention of the will of Allah.

Other religious believers, however, see a degree of distinction between their religious and ethical standpoints. While some people see their religious and ethical duties as compatible – and even co-extensive – they see distinct religious and ethical reasons for them. For example, some people see adultery as wrong because it is forbidden by God's law and because it involves deceiving marriage partners. Some, on the other hand, think of their religious and ethical duties as relating to different aspects of their lives, so they consider they have religious duties to pray and serve God, and ethical duties to pay taxes and train fares.

Not surprisingly, most atheists regard ethics as quite separate from religious beliefs. They see themselves as subject to ethical demands, but regard them as logically and culturally independent of religious belief – as we shall see later in this chapter.

Religion as the basis of ethics

Religious belief can of course provide a powerful basis for ethics. If people believe that the force that creates and sustains the universe gives them guidance on how to behave, and if they see this force as a personal being with whom they have a personal and emotional relationship, their convictions about what they ought to do are likely to be held very strongly. These convictions are also likely to be strengthened further because they see them as part of the truth about the whole of existence and their place within it. Religion gives them a world-view that has emotional and intellectual coherence and a sense of purpose: as individuals they know who they are, where they are intended to go, and where to look for guidance on their journey. Within this framework the guidance of their god, or gods, whether by direct revelation or through sacred texts and priests, may take the form of rules they should adhere to (what duties to perform, how to treat their fellow men and women etc.) or of goals they should aim for (such as spiritual enlightenment, a good relationship with God or a place in the after-life).

There are, of course, disagreements as to which religious world-view is the correct one and so which gives correct guidance. These disagreements occur not only between the major religious traditions but within them: in Buddhism there are the *theravada* and *mahayana* paths to enlightenment; in Christianity Catholic and Protestant views of the individual's relationship with God; and in Islam, Sunni and Shia accounts of how the faithful should behave. Within most religious traditions there are also fundamentalist and liberal schools of thought. Fundamentalists in Muslim, Christian and Jewish faiths tend to see good behaviour as a matter of obeying what they regard as the specific instructions of holy scripture, whereas liberals in the same religions consider they have freedom to make their own judgements on how to interpret religious guidance in specific circumstances. There are, of course, similar disagreements among people who see ethics as based on secular considerations.

One of the problems with basing ethics on a set of religious beliefs is that this provides no guidance for those who do not share those beliefs. People who do not believe in a particular god or in any god have no reason to accept a god's authority. Because of this problem, many have sought a basis for ethics in what they consider to be indisputable facts rather than in religious beliefs that not everyone shares. The hope is that if there is an ethical view that can be shown to be based on facts, the truth of which everyone accepts, then everyone will have a compelling reason for accepting it, and this will be to the benefit of us all. We will see later whether this quest has been successful.

Does ethics need religion as its basis?

Many people cannot see how those who have no religious belief can have a firm basis for ethical convictions. This is not surprising since, for thousands of years, most people have lived in societies dominated by religious traditions in which one or more gods have been the authority on how people should live. Consequently, many people think that if you have no religious beliefs you can have no source for your ideas of what is right and wrong.

Moreover, since most religions offer eternal rewards for living in certain ways, some people think that if you have no religious beliefs you will have no incentive for behaving well – or for bothering with morality at all. Why put up with the irksome restrictions of ethics if you get no reward for doing so?

And unless you see people and the environment as part of a god's creation why should you respect or value them?

Unsurprisingly, atheists challenge these ideas, claiming that their secular ethical convictions have firm foundations. Many consider, for example, that they do not need to see other people as created by a god in order to have good reasons to promote their well-being: their experience of the suffering and happiness of themselves and of people close to them is sufficient to convince them of the value of striving for the well-being of all. Moreover, they see this experience as something that is factual and demonstrably real, and not reliant on beliefs that may be questioned. Many atheists also claim that, though they regard the universe as the product of impersonal physical forces rather than created by a god, this in no way prevents them from admiring its beauty and complexity, nor from valuing people and nature as the product of these forces.

What non-religious bases of ethics are there?

As already mentioned, people have sought ethical guidance in what they see as indisputable facts – facts about nature, facts about human beings or facts about the way we think of ourselves. Unfortunately, as we shall see, these 'facts' usually turn out to be disputable, since they are either beliefs as to the facts – beliefs that not everyone shares – or a selection of facts that lead to particular conclusions, when a different selection might lead to different conclusions. Moreover, sometimes ethical views that claim to be based on objective 'facts' are really based on unacknowledged values that are built into the 'facts'.

We look first at attempts to base ethics on 'facts' about nature.

Nature as the factual basis of ethics

The ancient tradition that nature can teach us how we ought to live is so strong that for many people to say something is 'unnatural' is enough to imply that it is wrong. They see what is 'unnatural' as wrong and what is 'natural' as right. If one takes this approach it is obviously important to identify indisputable factual criteria by which to distinguish between 'natural' and 'unnatural' activities and situations.

One criterion frequently used is that human activities that interfere with natural processes are 'unnatural' and thus wrong. However, since no one can seriously maintain that all interference with natural processes (e.g. cooking food or bathing a wound) is wrong, we need an objective basis for drawing a line between interference that is permissible and impermissible. Where people draw this line, however, usually depends upon what they are used to: they are likely to regard activities they are familiar with as acceptable interference with nature and those they are not used to as unacceptable. Many people, for example, regard the use of antibiotics as acceptable interference with natural processes, but see innovative life-support techniques as unacceptable, even though, biologically at least, they interfere less than antibiotics with 'natural processes'. Basing the distinction between acceptable and unacceptable interference on what one is used to is to rely on subjective criteria: criteria that are relative to one's particular customs, culture and experience, and not criteria based on objective facts of nature.

Another appeal to the 'facts' of nature as the basis of ethics requires us to see nature as a goal-orientated, purposive system in which the various components have specific functions to perform; by carrying out their specific functions these components enable the goals of the whole system to be achieved. On this view human activities that use the components of nature for their specific functions are seen as acceptable, whereas those that use them for other purposes are not. For example, it is often claimed that the specific function of human sexual activity is reproduction of the species, and so it is only acceptable to use our sexuality for this purpose, whereas oral or same-sex activity – which cannot carry out this function – is unacceptable.

Seeing nature in this way raises two questions. First, is it an indisputable fact that nature is a goal-orientated, purposive system in which the various components have specific functions to perform? Second, even if it is accepted that nature is a purposive system, does it necessarily follow that each of its various components (e.g. human sexuality) has only one specific function?

So far as the first question is concerned, the view of nature as a goal-orientated, purposive system is challenged by many scientists and non-scientists. Many, for example, see natural processes – such as changes in species – simply as the outcome of physical forces and not as the unfolding of a purposeful 'master plan' that is aiming to achieve intended objectives. They consider that these physical interactions and the forces that cause them are non-mental, so they do not 'intend' anything. Consequently they do not see 'components' of nature, such as sexuality, as 'intended' to fulfil specific functions, nor that they should be used only for certain purposes. On their view the facts are that sexuality – as it is currently evolved – can be used in various ways, one of which results in the reproduction of the species, and so the facts do not in themselves indicate that it should be used in only one way.

So far as the second question is concerned, even if one sees nature as a purposive system, and accepts that reproduction is *one* specific function and purpose of sexuality, does an impartial and objective observation of the 'facts' of nature necessarily lead to the conclusion that this is its *only* function and purpose? It is, after all, a fact that the shapes of human and animal organs are such that they can be used for different types of sexual activity – oral and homosexual. They can also be used in heterosexual congress when the female is no longer fertile. They can, therefore, be used in ways that cannot lead to reproduction, and observations of animal behaviour show that members of many species frequently use them in these ways. So even if we see nature as a system in which components have specific functions, might there not be several purposes for sexuality – including giving pleasure and strengthening bonds in various types of relationship?

From an objective observation of the *facts* of nature alone it is, then, not clear that some uses of sexuality are 'natural' and others 'unnatural'. This being so, any claimed distinction between the acceptable and unacceptable uses of sexuality must be justified by appealing to other factors, such as values or beliefs. One belief frequently found to underlie such a distinction is that nature is created by a mind – a god – which (or who) intends sexuality to be used in only one way. But if this belief is the foundation of people's ethical views on sexuality, they should not claim to base them on an allegedly factual distinction between 'natural' and 'unnatural' uses.

Human nature as the factual basis of ethics

People identify and select different facts about human nature as the basis for ethics.

Aristotle, who lived in the fourth century BC, thought that there are three basic parts to our nature: physical, emotional and rational. He argued that to live in accord with our natures we should aim to live a life in which these three are properly exercised and fulfilled, so we should aim to have a fit body, an active mind and an emotionally fulfilled life. Human well-being for him consisted in achieving the right balance between these three parts.

Other thinkers, such as Jeremy Bentham and John Stuart Mill, have seen it as natural to humans to desire happiness or pleasure above all else. From this they have concluded that when we have a choice of actions, rather than aim simply for our own well-being, we should aim for the greatest amount of happiness or pleasure and the least amount of pain and suffering for as many people as possible. Our ethical decisions should be based on calculations as to how to achieve this.

There are, however, different views as to the type of happiness or pleasure people naturally seek. Is it a worry-free and blissful state of calm; a sense of achievement that comes from having fulfilling physical, emotional and intellectual involvement with others; the pleasures of a person of educated tastes; or the life of someone who feels in charge of their own destiny? These are just some of the ideas of what it is we all naturally desire and should aim for. None of them, however, can be taken as an objective fact of human nature since they reflect the cultures and tastes of the people who put them forward. When John Stuart Mill, for instance, claimed that the pleasures people would desire if they had the opportunity to do so would be those of educated people, he is referring to the pleasures of educated middle-class people in nineteenth-century Britain.

Another 'fact' about humans that is sometimes taken as a guide to ethics is the claim that we are social animals. Because we are naturally gregarious, so the claim goes, we should act in ways that enable societies to flourish. Some people maintain, for example, that for societies to flourish their members must be able to rely on each other telling the truth and keeping their promises. All humans should, therefore, accept truth telling and promise keeping as basic duties and, from these, develop a structure of social ethical obligations. But what these obligations should be depends upon the type of society considered most likely to promote human well-being. Different views have been put forward about this; we'll look at just two examples. Plato, writing in the fourth century BC, thought that, above all else, we need a society that is stable. For this we need everyone to stick to clear and specified duties that suit their individual aptitudes. Marx, on the other hand, writing in the nineteenth century, thought humans would only flourish in a society in which they were free to develop all aspects of their natures by engaging in many different activities.

In contrast to these ideas, some people have suggested that to ascertain what is natural to humans we must observe what the majority of humans do. They consider that what most people do is 'natural', whereas what just a few people do is 'unnatural' and a 'perversion' of true human nature. One difficulty with this approach is that what most people do varies from culture to culture and decade to decade. Consequently this guide to ethical behaviour turns out to be not what the majority do 'in nature', but what the majority *within a particular culture* appear to do when observed at a particular time.

Even if we disregard this problem, it remains difficult to claim that an activity is unnatural and wrong simply because it is done by only a minority, unless we are prepared to condemn all minority activities; but no one is prepared to do this. People who, for example, claim that homosexual activity is a perversion of our natures because only a minority of people engage in it do not condemn all minority activities – such as collecting train numbers, or being a concert pianist or a neurosurgeon – in the same way. They must therefore have values or beliefs other than the fact that it is a minority activity for condemning homosexuality.

Some people have based ethics on the needs and wants of humans. They see it as a fact that humans have certain natural needs (i.e. needs that are essential to their basic well-being as human beings) and they think we should all meet those needs. However, there is a vast variety of needs and wants that different people regard as essential. What is essential to the well-being of people in one culture may not even be desired by people in another. Moreover, 'essential' needs vary through time, as conditions, social and economic arrangements and technologies change. It is therefore difficult to claim that there is a set of essential needs that remain static through time or that all people have at any one time. Furthermore, the needs and wants of one person may conflict with each other and with those of other people, and the totality of people's needs often exceeds the resources available to satisfy them. Consequently, decisions have to be made as to which needs should be satisfied and which should not. This involves finding criteria for categorising some needs as more natural or more essential than others. It is at this point that purely factual and objective criteria become difficult to identify, and subjective or cultural values once again enter the considerations. This issue is looked at more fully in Chapter 6.

In the previous two sections we have seen that the deep-seated and ancient convictions that we should live in accord with the 'facts' of nature or human nature should be viewed with scepticism, since they depend on people building values and beliefs into what they see as the 'facts'. It is these *values* and *beliefs*, rather than *objective facts* of nature or human nature, that give them their guide to behaviour. Since everyone does not share these values and beliefs, these views do not base ethics on facts that everyone must accept.

Ideas of ourselves as the basis of ethics

A different approach to finding a secular basis for ethics, which is influential today, was developed by Immanuel Kant in the eighteenth and nineteenth centuries. Instead of basing ethics on claimed facts about nature or human nature Kant based it on what he thought were facts about how we think of ourselves. He said that we all hold certain ideas about ourselves and so should accept the ethical views that follow logically from them. These are ideas about freedom of choice: according to Kant we all think we have (sometimes, at least) the freedom and capacity to decide how we ought to behave. We have experiences of 'making up our minds' – that is, experiences of deciding for ourselves what we ought to do by the light of our own reasoning.[2]

Kant claims that, as mature individuals, not only do we think we *have* the capacity to do this but we also *value* this capacity and the freedom to use it. We regard this capacity as one of our most important attributes, considering that it gives us the dignity and worth of being morally responsible for what we do. He claims that since we value this capacity in ourselves we must value it in others, otherwise we would be inconsistent and irrational. And since we also value our ability to reason we must, he thinks, regard such inconsistency and irrationality as unacceptable.

He then argues that valuing the capacity of others to reason and make their own ethical decisions gives us certain obligations towards them. We should, for instance, respect their autonomy by respecting the decisions they make. We should also not tell them lies, because if we lie we thereby try to influence what they decide, instead of respecting their decisions based on circumstances as they truly are. We should also not break our promises to others since to do so deceives them rather than respects their intelligence.

Using these lines of argument Kant tries to show that we should all accept that there are certain types of act, such as truth telling and being honest, which we should always carry out, and others, such as breaking promises, which we should never carry out. He tries to give an indisputable basis for the conviction which many people have that certain types of act – such as truth telling and keeping promises – are intrinsically valuable and should be carried out irrespective of their consequences.

Although Kant claims these ethical views follow from the ideas we all have of ourselves, people have questioned whether we all do in fact think in this way. They claim that, although many people in western, secular and Protestant Christian cultures think they have the capacity and responsibility for making moral decisions by the light of their own reasoning, and put a high value on doing so, many people in other cultures consider their moral obligation is to be obedient to an external authority rather than develop their own views.

Intuitions as the basis of ethics

So far we have looked at examples of people finding ethical guidance in the beliefs and ideas they hold – whether these are religious beliefs or ideas about facts. Sometimes, however, people have intuitions about what is right and wrong, good or bad. They do not derive these intuitions from other beliefs or ideas, but just have an immediate conviction – a feeling of total certainty – as to what is right and wrong: the truth of their conviction seems self-evident to them. So people who have, for example, an intuition that human happiness is valuable will see no need to support it by making any general claims about human nature. Similarly, people who have intuitions that certain types of act – such as truth telling or promise keeping – are right see no need to support their intuitions by appealing to other beliefs. As a result of these intuitions the former may think people should try to produce as much human happiness as possible, and the latter that people should never lie or break promises.

Sometimes, too, people have ethical intuitions about a specific situation (i.e. they are convinced that a particular course of action is the right thing to do in a particular situation). From these intuitions they try to develop general ethical guidelines, on the grounds that if something is the right thing to do in one situation it may also be the right thing to do in similar situations. However, they often regard intuitions about particular situations as more important than the general guidelines. So if they have intuitions that are incompatible with any guidelines they have developed, they may well give priority to their latest intuitions. As a result, ethical views arising from this approach can vary radically.

While these 'self-evident' intuitions may provide a basis for ethics for the people who have them, they give no reasons to those who do not have them to adopt the same ethical views.

Emotions as the basis of ethics

Sometimes people base their ethical views on emotional experiences they have had. So someone who has witnessed the suffering of war victims may become a pacifist and someone who has felt fulfilled by parenthood may consider that assisting fertility should be a priority for healthcare resources. People may take one or two emotional experiences as the foundation of their ethical thinking and try to work towards general ethical views but, of course, others who have not had these experiences may not share their views.

This approach is very different from that of simply regarding whatever emotion one happens to have from moment to moment as the guide to what one should do. Since people's emotions can vary enormously, a moment-to-moment approach can lead to erratic and inconsistent viewpoints. For example, someone who at one time feels horror at the suffering caused by war, and so thinks war is wrong, may at another time be so angered by the aggression of one country against another that he feels the aggressors should be bombed. Consequently people are unlikely to develop coherent ethical views by simply accepting *all* their emotions-of-the-moment as the authority on what they should do. They need some more general guidance by which to decide which emotions should have priority, or even whether their emotions should be ignored altogether. Moment-to-moment emotions cannot provide an adequate basis for ethics.[3]

In this chapter we have looked at different evaluative standpoints from which people judge behaviour right or wrong, acceptable or unacceptable. We have also looked briefly at the various foundations on which people base their ethical views. In the next chapter we ask whether any of these foundations can be shown to be the one true basis of ethics that everyone should accept. We then consider the implications for ethics in the professions of the answer to this question.

Questions

Before going on to the next chapter, you may want to reflect on the points raised in this one.

1. Note down any activities you can think of that are:

    (a) legally permissible, but which you consider immoral

    (b) illegal, but which you consider morally acceptable.

2. If you are a member of a religion, note down any views of your religion with which you disagree.

3. If you have a political affiliation, note down any views of its general political standpoint with which you disagree.

4. Look over your reponses to the above questions.

   (a) In each case where you disagree with another standpoint, try to explain your reasons for disagreeing.

   (b) Are there any similarities in your reasons for disagreeing? If so, what values/convictions/principles does that indicate as being in your personal ethical standpoint?

5. Do you ever base any of your personal judgements on any of the secular views outlined in this chapter?

Notes

1   Since members of professions have to work within the law, when they are considering what they ought to do they must take into account any legal requirements and restrictions upon them. This book is a guide to ethics, not law, and readers should not see it as indicating what is legally permissible and impermissible.

2   Kant accepts that the way we think of ourselves may not be true (i.e. he accepts that we may not actually have the freedom we think we have). Nonetheless he thought it a fact that we *think* of ourselves as having some freedom of choice over our actions.

3   More is said about emotions in relation to ethics in Chapter 9.

Chapter 2

Seeking a Foundation
for Ethics in the Professions

In Chapter 1 we looked at various bases upon which people build their ethical views. In this chapter we ask whether any of these should be adopted by the professions as the one true basis for ethics.

Can any source or foundation of ethics be established as the true one?

We start addressing this question by looking at the sorts of causes and reasons that result in individuals accepting a particular basis for their ethics.

People can often explain why they as individuals accept a particular basis for ethics. They may point to particular causes – such as experiences and emotions they have had – or to particular reasons or beliefs they hold, which result in them accepting a certain basis for ethics.

Pointing to *causes and experiences* they might say:

> I was brought up in a God-fearing family and so have always seen the will of God as my moral authority.

or

> I used to see Marxism as the basis of moral values until I became disillusioned with the reality of communist regimes. Now I think we should just do what we can to relieve immediate poverty and to improve people's lives at a practical level, and not aim for some utopian ideal state.

or

> I used to think 'an eye for an eye and a tooth for a tooth' but, after witnessing the endless destruction that goes on when people adopt a policy of 'just retribution', I became convinced that it is more important not to harm others than to seek retribution.

Pointing to *reasons and beliefs* they might say:

> Since human beings need to live in societies I think we should base ethics on what promotes the well-being of societies.

or

> Because I believe God is good and omniscient I can see no better source of ethical guidance.

It is, however, one thing for individuals to identify the causes, reasons or beliefs behind why they accept a particular basis for their ethical guidance, and quite another to convince everyone else that they too should accept that basis.

Consider the following scenarios.

> A believes that there is a good and omniscient god who tells humans how they ought to behave. People who do not believe in a god will obviously not be swayed by A's views. They might, of course, come to believe in such a god, but if they don't A will have no arguments by which to convince them that they should accept the same basis for ethical guidance as he does.

> B is convinced that Marxist analysis of the effects of economic and social forces is true, so she thinks people can never have fulfilled lives in capitalist societies. All her ethical judgements are based on the importance of freeing people from the chains of capitalism. People who regard Marxist analysis as flawed will have no reason to accept the same basis for their ethical ideas.

> The ethical starting point for C, an atheist, is her conviction that happiness is the most valuable thing humans can strive for. C's conviction carries no weight for people who believe the most important goal for humans is to develop a good relationship with their god.

> The bases for D's views are his intuitions about which acts are right and wrong. He considers that the rightness of telling the truth and

wrongness of lying are self-evident and need no further justification. Consequently if other people do not have the same intuitions he cannot give them reasons why they should accept his convictions as the basis for their ethical views.

The basis for E's views is his experience as a US soldier in Iraq. Having seen the suffering of non-combatants, he considers that the killing of innocent people can never be justified. But, however hard he tries to convey the horror of what he saw, he may not be able to convince others that modern methods of warfare can never be justified.

These scenarios are somewhat oversimplified, but they indicate the difficulty of convincing everyone that they should accept a particular basis for their ethical views.

In Chapter 1 we also saw that people reject views allegedly derived from the 'facts' of nature or human nature because they do not accept the particular perceptions or selections of facts on which the views are based. We saw, too, that people challenge the Kantian view that ethics follows logically from how all human beings think, on the grounds that everyone in all cultures does not think in that way.

Since reasons, causes or experiences cannot be found that everyone will find compelling for accepting any particular basis of ethics, *no one source or foundation can be universally established as the true basis.*

While this conclusion may disappoint those who want certainty, it has important implications for the basis of professional ethics, as the next section explains.

Implications for ethics in the professions 1

Since no source or foundation can be universally established as the one true basis of ethics, those professionals – such as teachers and nurses – who do not explicitly represent any particular secular or religious viewpoint have no acknowledged grounds to claim any as the true basis. On the other hand, professionals who *do* represent particular viewpoints – such as priests, rabbis, gurus and mullahs – may have acknowledged grounds for stating that a particular basis of ethics is the true one for them. Because of this difference, some of the points made in this book do not apply to them.

Since 'non-representative' professionals have no acknowledged grounds for claiming any particular basis of ethics as the true one, they should not base their ethics on any one of them. To do so would be to lack the integrity (i.e. the honesty and transparency) expected of professionals.[1] To do so would also damage their role as professionals, for reasons we will now consider.

In the Introduction, professions were described as organisations and associations whose members deploy their expertise and powers to promote objectives valuable both for the individuals who receive their services and for the society in which they operate. These objectives include health (medicine), social care (welfare services), justice and education. To fulfil this role successfully in culturally complex societies professions must operate so that their services are equally available and appropriate to members of all cultures and traditions. If they were to adopt a particular religious or secular basis for their ethical values, and were to acknowledge doing so, people who did not share the same viewpoint might feel alienated and fear that these professions would not serve their interests. By adopting a particular basis, professionals would in effect be saying that the values of that religious or secular perspective were appropriate for their work with people of all perspectives. Moreover, if they claimed a particular viewpoint as the true basis of ethics, even though it cannot be demonstrated to be so, people might question their honesty and lose trust in them. This trust is essential if professionals are to work successfully with people from all cultures and traditions.

For all people to seek the services of professionals with the confidence that they will be dealt with fairly, they need to know that the values of 'non-representative' professions are *not* drawn from any particular cultural, ideological, religious or personal viewpoint.

The difference between 'representative' and 'non-representative' professionals is sometimes unclear when members of apparently 'non-representative' professions – such as teachers – are employed by organisations with specific religious or secular values, such as schools affiliated to a particular faith. In such cases the organisations for which they work should clarify the values upon which such professionals base their work. Faith schools, for example, should make clear whether the primary objective of their teachers is to indoctrinate (i.e. to inculcate the views of one faith) or to educate (i.e. to ensure pupils also understand other beliefs and value systems). They should also make clear whether pupils' work is assessed on its academic value or on the accuracy with which it reflects a particular viewpoint. Professionals in such organisations can act with integrity, and members of the public can have confidence and trust in them, only if the values on which they operate are made clear both within the organisation and to those who seek its services.

Of course, individual members of non-representative professions may have personal ethical views and values that are based on a particular religious or secular foundation, and that they live by in their personal lives. That is different, however, from them basing their professional practice on these particular values. (We consider the relationship between the personal and professional values of members of professions in Chapter 7.)

These considerations bring us to the question 'If it is inappropriate for non-representative professions in culturally complex democracies to base their ethics on any particular religious or secular foundation, what alternative is there?'

Is there a correct and true account of what is right and wrong?

Although it is not possible to establish any particular basis of ethics as the true one, might there not be a particular account of ethics – that is, a particular set of ideas of what is right and wrong (e.g. 'abortion is wrong', 'telling the truth is right') – which can be shown to be true, irrespective of the competing bases for ethics that people claim for them? If it can be shown that there are such true ideas, then professions can simply ensure that their members adhere to them, and can disregard concerns about the basis of ethics. But are there such demonstrably true ideas of what is right and wrong?

As young children most of us are brought up to think there are. We are led to believe, for example, that it is *true* that telling lies or breaking promises is wrong, and it is not just an opinion that our parents or our community happen to hold. Many people – known as objectivists – maintain that this is a correct view of ethics, and that there are objective truths about what is right and wrong that apply to all people at all times. Many others, however – known as relativists – contend that there are no such ideas and that to search for them shows a misunderstanding of the nature of ethics. We will now look at these two views – beginning with relativism – and then consider their implications for ethics in the professions.

Relativism

Relativists consider that since people's ideas of what is right and wrong vary according to their society, culture or individual inclinations, what we call ethics is merely the sum total of these cultural and individual opinions. For relativists, statements about what is right and wrong express opinions, not truths – opinions as to what is regarded as acceptable or unacceptable in particular groups or societies or by particular individuals. Moreover, they think that if we were to attempt to find a 'correct' account of ethics by analysing everyone's opinions and trying to find a common core, we would still end up with an opinion – namely, our opinion of what this analysis showed.

On their view we cannot escape from ethical opinion into the sunlit uplands of objective ethical truth because we cannot escape from being subject to the personal and cultural influences upon us. Since our views are the result of these influences and our reactions to them, we cannot 'step outside' our opinions. Even if in some ideal realm there were an objectively true and correct account of ethics, we would be able to perceive it only from the perspective of our particular biased and cultural situation: we could never give an unbiased or objective description of it. Consequently no one can ever claim to have 'opinion-free', objective, true and correct ideas of what is right and wrong that should be adhered to by everyone. From this it follows that no one is ever justified in imposing their ethical views on anyone else on the grounds that it is 'the truth'. Everyone should therefore be tolerant of, and respect, the ethical opinions of others. Even though individuals may be convinced that their own views are the true ones, they should realise that this is merely their opinion.

Some people who accept this relativist view of ethics have concluded that it justifies them in ignoring ethics altogether. After all, why should they put up with the limitations that ethics imposes on them – telling them what to do and what not – if these demands are just a matter of opinion? People who think in this way are known as ethical nihilists (*nihil* is a Latin word meaning 'nothing'). According to them the idea that we have ethical obligations is an illusion, and ideas of what is right and wrong are fantasies, rather like Santa Claus.

Most relativists, however, disagree with this. They consider that although no account of ethics can claim to be objectively true (i.e. true for all people at all times) it does not follow that individuals have no ethical obligations. On the contrary, they consider that we all have obligations that are relative to individuals in their particular time and situation.

CHALLENGES TO RELATIVISM

The following four challenges to relativism have been put forward:

1. It is inconsistent.
2. It has unacceptable consequences.

3.   It denies people can ever really mean what they do mean.

4.   There are no logically compelling reasons to accept it.

We will now look at each of these in turn.

The first challenge is that the relativist position is internally inconsistent, for when relativists assert that everyone should be tolerant of the ethical opinions of others they seem to be saying both that no one should impose their views on anyone else *and* that everyone should behave in the way that relativists think is right (i.e. that everyone should be tolerant of the ethical views of others). But what about people who think that it is wrong to tolerate the view that ethnic cleansing is sometimes right? Relativists themselves would want to impose their ideas on such people.

The second challenge is that the relativist position on tolerance has unacceptable consequences, since it seems to imply that we should allow others to do whatever they think is right. But what if people think it right to use brute force to prevent others from acting in accordance with their ethical convictions? Aren't there times when we *are* ethically entitled to oppose others doing what they think is right? If one section of the human race considers it is justified in carrying out genocide on another should we not try to stop it?

A third challenge to relativism is that if, as it claims, there are only opinions and no truths in ethics, we can never assert that anything really is right or really is wrong. So if someone says, for example, 'genocide is wrong', their assertion does not really mean that genocide truly is wrong, only that they think it is wrong or that the prevailing view in their culture is that it is wrong. For the relativist, the speaker cannot be saying it is actually true that genocide is wrong, because there are no ethical truths. Similarly, if a group of people are arguing about whether fox hunting is morally acceptable, for the relativist they are not really talking about the rightness and wrongness of fox hunting itself, only telling each other their opinions of fox hunting. Some people find this analysis of the meaning of ethical statements unacceptable. As they see it, people really do think, and really do mean to say, that certain things – such as fox hunting and genocide – are *in fact* wrong, and that if anyone disagrees with this, their view is incorrect.

A fourth challenge to relativism is that there is no logically compelling argument to accept it since it does not follow from the fact that people have different ethical opinions that there cannot be ethical truth. The simplest way to explain this point is by analogy. In the past, people had different opinions about the shape of the earth – some thought it flat, others spherical

– but it did not follow from this that the earth had no shape. The situation was simply that no one could find sufficient evidence to convince everyone of the earth's true shape. So, on this analogy, it does not follow solely from the fact that people have different opinions about ethics that there can be no ethical truth. There *could be* such a thing as ethical truth but we just cannot establish what it is. According to this argument, even though people have different opinions of what is right and wrong, it is possible that there is an objectively true and correct account of ethics. So it is not illogical both to accept that people have different opinions and to hold an objectivist view of ethics. We will now turn to the objectivist view.

Objectivism

In traditional monocultural societies people generally regard the ethical views of their society as correct and true. Such objectivism was particularly strong when people were less conscious than they are now of different cultures, but it is still powerful in societies where most people look to one source for ethical guidance – in strongly Catholic, Shia or Sunni societies, for example. In less culturally monolithic societies, individuals who have complete trust in what they see as the basis of ethics also have strong convictions about the objective truth of their ethical views. Many people who consider, for example, they know the truth about their god's wishes, or who think they have a correct view of human nature, are certain they have an unimpeachable source of truth about how humans ought to behave.

However, just as we have seen that it is not possible to find reasons or causes everyone will find compelling for accepting a particular basis of ethics as the true one, so it is not possible to find reasons everyone will find compelling for accepting a particular account of ethics as the true one. Imagine the impossibility of convincing people of all religious and secular traditions that polygamy or remarriage after divorce is wrong, or that euthanasia or abortion – even if performed only in certain circumstances – is right. And, as we have also seen, relativists would not only be unconvinced by claims that anything really is right or wrong, but would regard such claims as based on a misconception of ethics.

Implications for ethics in the professions 2

The implications for the professions of these views on the relativity and objectivity of ethics can be appreciated by remembering that the aim of (non-representative) professions in culturally complex societies is to achieve objectives – such as health, safe communities and education – for all sections of society. To achieve these objectives, members of a profession must subscribe to at least a minimal set of ethical views and values they share with colleagues. There are several reasons for this.

First, the work of a profession would be self-defeating if its members operated according to different basic ethical agendas. For example:

> If some teachers thought it right to grade students' work by impartially applying academic criteria while others considered they should give whatever grades would make the students feel good about themselves, the value of assessment would be destroyed and communal trust in educational grading systems would be undermined.

> Some time ago there was a move in the English police service to develop a statement of ethics. At one point it was suggested that part of the statement should include the assertion that the service would support any officer acting in accord with his or her conscience. It was, however, soon realised that it would be impossible to operate a police service that had made this commitment, since all sorts of different and incompatible ideas of right and wrong might exist in the consciences of individual officers, especially as they are recruited from all sections of British society. As a result, they might pursue incompatible objectives.

Second, as already mentioned, if a profession is not seen to adhere to known ethical values or to strive for known objectives that people regard as worthwhile, they will not seek its services. Clients, potential clients and the general public need to know the fundamental values and objectives of a profession, and be able to trust that its members adhere to them.

Third, to be effective a profession needs the goodwill of the society in which it operates, and it will only have this if its members strive to comply with values that are generally thought to be in the interests of the society as a whole. Whenever there are public inquiries and whenever members of professions are held accountable to the public for the decisions they make, they are expected to pay heed to such values.

From these considerations we see that when individuals are acting as members of a profession they cannot take a totally relativist view of ethics. They must be prepared to adhere to the shared ethical ideas of their profession and cannot regard themselves as entitled to adopt whatever ideas, values or principles they wish. Nor, when acting in a professional capacity, can they give limitless tolerance to the ethical views of others; they could not, for example, act in complicity with a client's commitment to anarchism if it cuts across the fundamental values of the society in which their professional relationship takes place.

Nor can members of professions take a completely objectivist view of ethics.[2] Since professionals must adopt the shared values of their profession they cannot regard their personal ethical convictions as the objective truth that they will stick to in professional practice irrespective of whether they are compatible with these shared values.

Nor should they claim that the shared ethical views of their profession are, in fact, the objective truth about ethics (i.e. true for all people at all times). Since reasons cannot be found that everyone would find compelling to accept a particular account of ethics as the true one, if professionals were to claim their shared values as the objective truth, this would call into question their integrity. It would also in effect condemn any different ethical views that people espouse in their personal lives.

So, instead of claiming that the ethical values of their profession are the objective truth for all people at all times, professionals should only claim that they are the appropriate values for their role as professionals in culturally complex democracies. In the next chapter we will see what these values are, and the justification for claiming that they are appropriate to the professional role.

The appropriate foundation for ethics in the professions

In this chapter we have seen that professions cannot operate without their members sharing certain general ethical values. We have also seen that non-representative professions in culturally complex democratic societies should not claim any particular religious or secular convictions as the true basis of ethics on which their professional values are founded, nor that their professional ethical views are true for all people at all times. This being so, the justification for the ethical values of (non-representative) professions in culturally complex democracies must be grounded on their *role* in those societies and not on any claims of objective ethical truth.

Questions

1. Do you think it important that members of your profession should work to the same basic values and objectives?

2. In so far as your profession has shared values and objectives, can you say what these are?

3.   What evidence have you for your answer to question 2 (e.g. observation of working practices, policy or vision statements, statements by professional bodies)?

4.   Are there any legal or professional requirements on members of your profession that are relevant to the issues in this chapter?

Notes

1   The integrity of professionals is discussed in Chapter 8.

2   In contrast with what is said here about 'non-representative' professions, it seems that, for example, part of the role of Catholic priests is to claim that Catholic values *are* true for all people at all times. Since this claim seems to be part of the shared values of their profession, there is no anomaly in them promulgating it.

Chapter 3

Values Integral to the Role of Professions

We have described the role of (non-representative) professionals as being to promote objectives that are valuable for the individuals with whom they work – students, patients, clients, members of the public, and so on. We have also said that professions are regarded as contributing to the well-being of culturally complex democracies so long as they strive to achieve these objectives for people in all sections of society. By providing things like health and social care, educational opportunities, a fair trial, decent living environments, safe communities for all, they promote the democratic ideal that all citizens are valued and respected.

What values must members of these professions subscribe to in order to fulfil this role successfully? When acting in their professional capacity they must value the fundamental objectives of their profession. As we saw in the last chapter, unless members of a profession share its basic values, the profession cannot operate successfully, and this obviously applies to valuing its objectives. No doubt professions have their own ways of identifying and describing what are their overall objectives, but as working models of what these are we can say that:

- health and social care professionals must value people's health and the relief of suffering
- police must value public order and people living in crime-free and safe communities
- architects and engineers must value people living in pleasant and safe built environments

- police, officers of the courts and lawyers must value people having the protection of the law, and the protection of their interests

- professionals in education must value people having opportunities to learn and develop skills

- accountants must value financial probity and the protection of their clients' financial interests

- veterinary professionals must value the well-being of animals (and their owners)

- ecologists must value the well-being of the natural environment and so on.

The overall purpose of these objectives is to promote the well-being of people. Even though professionals in veterinary and environmental work focus on the well-being of animals, plants and the biosphere, they nonetheless have a professional responsibility to consider the well-being of humans. In so far as all the objectives promote this well-being, members of every profession must value them all. So, for example, healthcare workers must value the objective of the police service to ensure that people live in safe communities and have the protection of the law. To this extent professionals have mutually supportive objectives and can collectively promote the social cohesion that culturally complex democracies need.

Because professionals value the objectives of their profession, they must obviously be concerned with the *results* of their actions (i.e. with the extent to which their actions promote these objectives and how they affect the well-being of people). Chapter 4 considers the demands that this obligation makes upon professionals.

Because their role is to provide services for all sections of society, professionals must also value treating everyone *fairly*. There are two ways in which they should do this. First, they should regard the well-being of people from all sections and groups in society as equally important. They should, for example, see it as wrong to discriminate between people because of their culture, race, gender or sexual orientation, and should treat them differently only if there are differences between them that are directly relevant to the professional situation. So, for example, a doctor should not treat patients differently because they are of different cultural membership but because they have different medical conditions. Second, they should treat people in ways that are just to them as individuals – that is, as is appropriate to their individual needs, to what they individually deserve and to any other relevant aspects of their individual situations.

One important aspect of individuals' situations is their wishes in connection with how they want to live and how they want to be treated. Indeed, it is an ideal of democracy that people should be as self-determining as possible, and the fact that citizens in democracies have some political self-determination by being able to vote underlies the view that democracy is a morally better system of government than totalitarianism. As valued institutions in democracies, professions are expected to uphold this ideal.

Professionals should, therefore, see value in respecting people's wishes and enabling them to be as *autonomous* as possible. For example, whenever appropriate, doctors should inform patients about alternative treatments and allow them to choose between them; and if researchers wish to involve people in their research projects they should do so only after receiving their voluntary and informed consent. Unless professionals accept the value of promoting and respecting the autonomy of everyone with whom they have professional relationships, they are likely to treat people unfairly by paying more attention to the wishes of those who are more assertive, educated or articulate. Chapters 5 and 6 look at the obligation of professionals to treat people fairly, and Chapter 7 at their obligation to respect autonomy.

Professionals can only carry out their role if they are trusted. They need people in general to trust that they will pursue the objectives of their profession, and they need individuals to trust that they will work for their particular interests. Professionals will not have this trust if they do not act with *integrity* (i.e. act in accordance with the values and objectives they purport to have as professionals). This involves keeping promises, having the appropriate expertise and fulfilling the other expectations implied by the claim to be professional. Chapter 8 considers the issues raised by the requirement that professionals act with integrity.

We can summarise the fundamental values integral to fulfilling the role of professionals in culturally complex democratic societies as:

- to value results that are the most beneficial and least harmful to individuals and to society
- to value treating individuals justly and fairly by not discriminating between them on irrelevant grounds, and by paying attention to their individual needs
- to value people's autonomy as far as possible within a society in which the legitimate interests of all must be considered

- to value integrity by acting in accord with the stated or implied values, undertakings and objectives of their profession.

How should values be related to professional practice?

There is a growing tendency to embed ethical values into professional practice by means of detailed codes, procedures and rules, with the result that 'behaving ethically' increasingly becomes a matter of rule following. But is this the best way to make professionals mindful of their ethical obligations? We look at two views of the general nature of ethical obligation and at the implications of these views for the professions.

The nature of ethical obligation in general

There is a strong tradition of seeing ethical obligation as a matter of obeying rules. This view is what many of us are given as young children: good girls and boys obey the rules. It is an attractive view, for if the rules are sufficiently precise we have an account of ethics and ethical obligation that is clear, authoritative and comforting – in that our only duty as individuals is to be obedient and we do not have the burden of thinking for ourselves. But to what extent is it tenable to see ethical obligation in this way?

If values are expressed as a set of rules and all we ever have to do is carry them out, the meaning of the rules must be precise. It must not be possible to interpret them in different ways otherwise we do not just have to obey, but to work out the best way to interpret them. 'Turn to the east and bow three times' leaves little room for interpretation, but what about 'Tell the truth'? Does it mean 'Tell the *whole* truth' or 'Never utter a lie' – or what? And should the rule always be understood in the same way in every situation? Consider the following scenario.

> A doctor is telling her patient about his condition. To 'tell the truth', must she inform the patient of everything she knows about the condition, including all possible and rare complications? If she considers that to mention these would needlessly worry the patient, can she omit them and still be regarded as having conformed to the rule? Will she still be telling the truth?
>
> Would whatever is necessary to 'tell the truth' in this situation be different from what would be necessary when the same doctor is lecturing medical students about the patient's condition?

Since the injunction to 'tell the truth' is not sufficiently precise for us to know exactly what to do in every situation, rules could not be as simple and general as this if ethical obligation were to be just a matter of obeying rules. The rules would have to make clear what people must do in various circumstances, including those when the rules clash. The doctor's situation above, for example, might be seen as involving a clash between the rule to 'tell the truth' and the rule to 'avoid unnecessary harm'.

Plato described a situation where rules clash: someone has borrowed an axe, promising to return it, but the owner of the axe has since become a manic murderer. Should the borrower obey the rule to keep a promise or the rule to prevent harm? To have a rule that we should always keep a promise whatever harm may occur would seem to many people to be both unrealistically inflexible and immoral – in fact, stupid! But if it is accepted that in some circumstances we should make exceptions to obeying a rule, and if our ethical obligation is to be obedient and not to think for ourselves, we need further rules to tell us which rules take precedence over which, and whether they should always have this priority. Should the rule to prevent unnecessary harm always take priority over the rules to tell the truth or to keep promises, for instance? And, if not, in what circumstances should it not?

The problem with seeing ethical obligation as obedience to rules is that, however complex the rules become, they will be unable to take account of all circumstances that can occur. So from time to time the rules will be inappropriate or inadequate. Considerations such as these lead many people to consider it unfeasible to see the ethical obligation of mature individuals who are inevitably involved in a wide variety of circumstances simply as obedience to rules. While they accept it may be useful to treat ethical obligation as obedience to rules when developing ethical awareness in the young, they consider that often – if not always – the ethical obligation of mature people must include an element of *judging* for themselves what they ought to do in particular circumstances.

The debate as to the nature of the ethical obligation is a very ancient one; there are strands in most religious traditions that support different views. Some Christian, Judaic and Muslim thinkers consider it is to be obedient. On their view we are told how to behave by God or His representatives and, since we can have no higher authority, we should obey divine instruction. A twentieth-century Christian expression of this view is given by Emil Brunner in *The Divine Imperative* (1947): 'There is no Good save obedient behaviour, save the obedient will... The Good consists in doing what God wills at any particular moment.'

There are, however, views in Buddhist, Judaic, Christian and Muslim thought that, from time to time at least, people must think for themselves. Such views hold that God has given us the capacity to reason and the freedom to use it in order to decide for ourselves what we ought to do. A Christian version of this is given by St Thomas Aquinas. In his *Summa Theologica*, written in the thirteenth century, he considers that 'conscience is the dictate of reason' and that 'the will which disobeys the reason...is always in the wrong' (in Gilby 1951, p.292).

In secular traditions from at least the fifth century BC – in China with the development of Confucian thought, and in Greece with the beginnings of western philosophy – importance has been given to individuals deciding for themselves what they ought to do. As we saw in Chapter 1, Immanuel Kant, writing in the eighteenth century, thought we should not carry out an action unless we are convinced *by the light of our own reasoning* that it is the right thing to do, for only then do we act with full moral responsibility and possess the dignity and worth of being a moral agent. He thought that when individuals act in order to be obedient to an external authority – whether a religious or secular one – they are motivated by a desire to obey that authority rather than a sense of ethical duty. On his view, to do what God wills out of obedience to Him is to be motivated by religious devotion, not by ethical concern, and, although such devotion may be admirable from a religious point of view, it has no ethical value.

Kant thought that as individual moral agents we have two levels of moral responsibility. We should not only decide what we ought to do in a particular situation, but also what ethical values to have in the first place. We should, for example, decide by the light of our own reasoning whether we value integrity, honesty, promise keeping, truth telling and so on, and then decide how to apply our values to our particular situation.

Twentieth-century existentialists, too, considered that individuals should choose their own ethical values. They held that we should reject *all* values, rules and principles from all sources whatsoever – God, our peers, culture, social customs, nature, reason and so on – and then choose from scratch which values to hold. Existentialists considered that people live in 'bad faith' if they simply accept 'given' values; they believed that individuals should regard themselves as the originators of whatever values they live by.

However, sociologists, psychologists and philosophers argue that people can never be totally free to decide their own values in this way, for two main reasons. First, it is impossible for any individual to grow up in a value-free vacuum: whatever community we are born into has values that influence our judgements and decisions. Even if we grow up in a group that rejects conventional standards, that group will prefer certain ways of behaving to others. Whether these preferences are based on high-minded ethical considerations or merely what is necessary for the 'survival of the gang', they give us values and rules we are required to live by – even if these values are only some version of 'honour among thieves'. Moreover, we cannot ever escape these given values completely. We cannot reach a position of having no values whatsoever and then decide what new values to adopt, because whatever efforts we make to do this will be influenced by the values of our background and current social context. Second, they point out that even if we could find ourselves in a 'value-free vacuum' we would not be able to decide from scratch which values to adopt; for, if we had no values whatsoever, we would have no reasons for regarding one activity or state of affairs as better or worse than any other. For example, if we did not already value human happiness more than human suffering, and held no other ethical views and values, we would have no reason for regarding torture as wrong.

Considerations such as these have led many people to the view that, although individuals cannot decide upon their ethical values from scratch, mature people are often in a position to reflect upon values they have absorbed from their backgrounds. They can, for instance, consider the relative importance of these values – whether, for example, honesty should always take precedence over any other value or whether dishonesty may ever be justified. They can also decide for themselves whether, in particular circumstances, they should set aside some values in favour of others. They can also reflect on how to interpret values – in what, for example, being truthful consists, or what integrity demands of them – and how to apply them to particular situations.

Today many people take the view that not only can mature individuals think in these ways but that they should do so as part of their moral responsibility. Within this view ethical values are seen as *general principles* rather than as *precise rules*. Since general principles lack precision, they allow individuals the scope to decide how to interpret and apply them to varying situations.[1]

The ethical obligation of members of professions

The situation of members of professions is generally more akin to that of mature people with a moral responsibility to reflect on ethical values rather than of children with a duty to be obedient to rules. Members of professions have expertise – a body of knowledge, experience and skills – that they are expected to deploy in relation to particular situations. To do so they must take into account all ethically relevant factors. These may include technical aspects of a situation, such as the relevant legislation or medical prognosis, the client's needs, and the general expectations that they as professionals will deal fairly with all parties and strive to achieve the best outcome. Making appropriate judgements in the light of all these considerations cannot be reduced to obeying a set of ethical rules. While professionals are not, as existentialists might hope, free to choose their values from scratch – since they should uphold the values integral to their role – they need some freedom to consider how to relate and apply these values to circumstances.

Portraying ethics in the professions as obedience to rules can have undesirable effects. People are tempted to try to find ways around rules and regulations: what they can 'get away with' while still technically conforming to them. Ethics then becomes a matter of adhering to the letter of the rule or law, rather than making judgements about how best to act in the spirit of ethical values. If this happens, when situations arise with which the rules do not quite 'fit', individuals are ill-prepared to make judgements about what they ought to do. As regulatory codes have proliferated in recent years, and as examples of unethical behaviour in professions have increasingly made the headlines, the cry has gone up that what is needed is fewer rules and a greater sense of individual moral responsibility among professionals.[2]

The sense of responsibility and the self-esteem of members of professions is likely to be greater if they see themselves as individuals who are trusted to decide how best to interpret and apply general ethical principles rather than as people required to obey rules.

Seeing ethical values as general principles is, of course, compatible with professional bodies and advisory groups drawing up recommendations on how they should normally be interpreted and applied. It is also compatible with professions developing more detailed protocols and advisory rules in relation to specific activities – such as storing data, obtaining informed consent, taking blood and using questionnaires. Such recommendations and advisory rules are suggested ways of putting the principles into practice. Recommendations about handling data are part of concern for the best results since they aim to prevent damage to research subjects through breaches of privacy, and protocols for obtaining informed consent are ways of respecting autonomy.

Understood in these ways, guidelines, rules and protocols do not take away the moral responsibility and autonomy of professionals, who still have to decide how general guidelines should be applied to their particular situation. Advisory rules only come into play once professionals have made the decision that it is right to carry out the procedures to which the rules apply. Moreover, while a protocol may provide, for example, a template for consent forms, professionals still have to decide whether they should adapt the form, bearing in mind all ethically relevant factors in the situation.

In the light of these considerations the values integral to successfully fulfilling the professional role are best seen as *four general principles*:

1. To seek results that are the most beneficial and least harmful to individuals and to society.

2. To treat individuals justly and fairly by not discriminating between them on irrelevant grounds and by paying attention to their individual needs.

3. To respect people's autonomy as far as possible within a society in which the legitimate interests of all must be considered.

4. To behave with integrity by acting in accord with the stated or implied values, undertakings and objectives of the profession.

By using these principles as the foundation of their statements of values and codes of conduct, professions adopt values that are essential to the successful fulfilment of their role in culturally complex democratic societies.

Some people may consider these principles deficient in that they do not include any reference to rights. This is omitted for two reasons. First, we are concerned here with identifying the ethical rather than legal obligations of professionals. So, while professionals should, of course, respect people's legal rights, this legal obligation is not appropriate for inclusion here. Second, the point that professionals should respect people's ethical or moral rights is not included here because any moral rights relevant to professionals can be derived from the principles already included. For example, the claim that everyone has a moral right to healthcare can be derived from the principles of treating people fairly and of seeking the best results for all. Consequently, by adopting the above four principles, professionals are already subscribing to values that underlie the moral rights relevant to their work. 'Respect moral rights' does not, therefore, need to be itemised as a separate ethical principle. If you wish to think more about rights at this point, turn to Chapter 12.

Some people may also feel these principles deficient in that they omit any reference to being caring and loving. Although this is important in some professions, it is omitted here because it gives little guidance as to what people should actually do unless it is interpreted in terms of the principles already in the framework. Being caring of others, for example, involves promoting their well-being, respecting their wishes and treating them justly.

In Part Two we explore the obligations the four principles give to members of professions.

Questions

1. Do you consider that members of your profession should subscribe to the four principles listed on p.53?

2. If you think they should not, what are your reasons for this?

3. Are any guidelines or statements of values issued by your profession compatible with some or all of these principles?

4. Are there any legal or professional requirements on members of your profession that are relevant to the issues in this chapter?

Notes

1   Regarding ethical values as principles in this way does not, however, exclude the possibility that sometimes there may be little need to interpret or reflect on them. When, for example, a rich person has promised to pay for a meal in a restaurant it is clear what she ought to do at the end of the meal – she has no need to reflect on how to interpret keeping a promise in that situation!

2   For example, in the 2002 Reith Lectures given on BBC Radio 4 by Onora O'Neill.

Part Two

Exploring Values

In Part One we identified values essential to fulfilling the role of professionals who work with people in all sections of culturally complex democracies. We have seen that these values are best expressed as the following four general principles:

1. To seek results that are the most beneficial and least harmful to individuals and to society.

2. To treat individuals justly and fairly by not discriminating between them on irrelevant grounds and by paying attention to their individual needs.

3. To respect people's autonomy as far as possible within a society in which the legitimate interests of all must be considered.

4. To behave with integrity by acting in accord with the stated or implied values, undertakings and objectives of the profession.

In Part Two we look at the obligations these principles can give to professionals. We shall come across situations where these obligations conflict – for example, when respecting a client's autonomy may damage the prospects of achieving the best results. We will note these conflicts and may consider ways of dealing with them in particular situations. In Part Three, Chapter 10 discusses general ways of addressing such conflicts.

In Part Two we also discuss two topics at greater length than might be expected. This is done to illustrate the sort of analysis that may be necessary when professionals consider which actions and policies are ethically appropriate. These topics are the ethics of compensation (discussed in Chapter 5) and respect for confidentiality and privacy (discussed in Chapter 8). If you do not want to consider these topics at the length presented, simply move on to a subsequent topic.

As you begin Part Two you are reminded that examples of situations are used to explore ethical issues and not to recommend ways of acting in particular circumstances. Nor do the examples identify legal or other requirements which are specific to particular professions. As a member of a profession you may have legal and statutory obligations. You may also be required to comply with professional guidelines, codes of conduct or regulatory procedures that relate to the situations and issues discussed here. When this is so, you must give precedence to these legal and professional requirements over any suggestions in this book. If you disagree with any of these requirements you can make your views known through formal channels provided by your profession.

Chapter 4

Seeking the Best Results

Producing benefits and preventing harm

We have expressed the principle concerned with results as 'to seek the results that are the most beneficial and least harmful to individuals and to society'. By expressing it in this way, the two aims of

1. producing as many benefits as possible

2. avoiding causing, or preventing, as much harm as possible

are seen as part of a single obligation. To fulfil this obligation professionals should consider both the amount of benefits and the amount of harm alternative courses of action might produce.

Some people, however, consider that the obligation to avoid causing harm is quite separate from the obligation to pursue benefits. They see causing harm as an intrinsically bad act that must be avoided at all costs, so the obligation to 'do no harm' should always take precedence over all others. For them, professionals have an overriding duty not to harm people affected by their work – be they clients, students, patients or members of the public. Some see this as an obligation to do no harm whatsoever, others as an obligation to do no gratuitous or unnecessary harm.

Those who take the first view may consider it is never permissible to take life, nor to cause any unhappiness, pain, suffering or loss of independence, and not to damage anything else they consider to be valuable. Those who take the second view consider that a proscription against causing any harm whatsoever would, in fact, lead to unacceptable results, since it is often impossible to achieve what is valuable without causing some harm. For example, it is sometimes impossible to cure someone of a life-threatening illness without treating them in a way that will impair their quality of life, either temporarily or permanently.

If people take the second view, they must decide whether the harm would be gratuitous or unnecessary by weighing the likely harm caused by an action against both the likely benefits it might produce and any other ethical demands it might satisfy. They might consider such questions as:

- Can the same benefits be achieved in some other way that does not cause harm? If not, are the benefits so great that they justify causing the harm?

- Is the action that causes harm the only way to meet other ethical demands (e.g. to treat people fairly)? If so, does that, on balance, justify causing the harm?

Given the impossibility of avoiding all harm in many professional activities that are considered valuable – either because of the benefits they achieve or other ethical demands they satisfy – it is both practical and ethically justified for professionals to interpret the obligation not to cause harm as an obligation not to cause unnecessary and gratuitous harm.

Once professionals adopt this interpretation of the obligation not to cause harm, it makes little practical difference whether they see it as a separate obligation from that of seeking the best results or as part of it. In either case, when deciding what they should do, they must weigh the importance of the obligation not to cause harm against their other obligations: to produce benefits, to treat people fairly, to respect their autonomy and to act with integrity. Consequently, for the sake of clarity, and at the risk of over-simplification – in this book the ethical demand not to cause harm is treated as part of the general obligation to seek the best results.

Promoting people's well-being

The obligation to seek the best results affects almost all decisions professionals make, since it obliges them to use whatever resources are at their disposal to pursue the most valuable consequences they can achieve. Resources do not just mean financial resources, but include:

- the time, energy and expertise of themselves and colleagues

- the time and energy of clients, students, patients and members of the public

- the goodwill of colleagues, the community, sponsors, and so on

- the facilities and reputation of the profession and organisations in which professionals work

- the opportunities provided by situations (e.g. the once-in-a-lifetime opportunity a student has to study, the one opportunity to use valuable research material).

Small-scale, everyday decisions – such as the amount of attention a nurse gives a particular patient, or a lecturer gives a student – as well as large-scale decisions about budget allocations, should take account of the principle to seek the best results. But what results should professionals regard as the best?

In the last chapter we saw that professionals should value the well-being of people. They should aim for results that most promote people's well-being, whether by bringing them benefits or by reducing or preventing harm to them.

Unsurprisingly, people have different views as to what human well-being consists of. Some see pleasure as the most important element in people's well-being, and think we should aim to bring about as much pleasure and as little pain to people as possible. If ever the pursuit of pleasure is likely to give rise to some pain we should try to produce the greatest balance of pleasure over pain. One person who held this view was Jeremy Bentham, an English thinker of the nineteenth century. He regarded all sources of pleasure as valuable, even those not normally highly respected: 'Prejudice apart,' he claimed, 'the game of pushpin [a simple board game] is of equal value with the arts and science of music and poetry' (Bentham 1843, p.253).

While many people like Bentham's approach because it does away with elitism and intellectual or cultural snobbery, others – including John Stuart Mill, writing just after Bentham – fear it could result in people aiming only for the most easily accessible pleasures, such as food, drink and sexual enjoyment, and not bothering with pleasures that are worthwhile but more difficult to obtain. Mill claimed that the element in human well-being with the greatest value does not lie in all pleasures, but in the pleasurable sense of fulfilment that comes from striving for something worthwhile. He thought this sense of self-fulfilment was valuable even when it could be reached only after considerable pain, or when the worthwhile objectives were only partially achieved. As he rather graphically puts it, 'better to be a human being dissatisfied than a pig satisfied' (Mill 1960, p.9).

Others have developed the view that the most essential element for people's well-being consists of the happiness of fulfilment experienced over a lifetime rather than in pleasure-filled moments. To strive for this we must, Aristotle suggested, develop our physical, emotional and intellectual capacities as fully as possible, thereby fulfilling every aspect of ourselves. The more we do this during the course of our lives, the happier and more worthwhile our lives will be.

John Rawls, in his *A Theory of Justice* (1971), argues that well-being consists in people being able to develop, revise, modify and live out their own life plans. Somewhat similarly, Richard Hare, in his book *Moral Thinking* (1981), considers it is important for people to be able to satisfy their preference as to how they wish to live. At its simplest, Hare's view is that the world is a better place the more people's preferences are satisfied and the less they are frustrated. So when deciding what to do, we should work out how the options open to us would affect everyone – including ourselves – and then consider how everyone would *prefer* to be affected and prefer *not to be* affected. We should carry out whichever option we think would satisfy as many preferences and frustrate as few – both now and in the future – as possible.

Many people also have notions of well-being that have specifically religious dimensions. They may consider, for instance, that people's well-being consists in participating in particular religious activities, or in fulfilling a role within a religious community. Others may see well-being as having a particular relationship with their god, or being in a certain spiritual state, or seeing death in a particular way.

Since there are these and many more views on what constitutes people's well-being, how should professionals set about seeking results that most promote it? There is a danger that they will impose their own ideas of well-being on others. This being so, when deciding what to do to aim for the best results, professionals should:

- use their expertise to estimate as *objectively* as possible the likely effects on all who may be affected by their actions
- be *sensitive* to the perspectives of the people affected by taking into account what they see as important to their own well-being and how they might view the acceptability of those effects
- assess how actions are likely to affect people in the long term.

In doing this, professionals should strive to be impartial by regarding the well-being of everyone as equally important. They should not, for example, give greater weight to the interests of people whose cultures are similar to their own, or to people with whom they feel particular affinity or sympathy. Instead, they should be concerned to maximise the well-being of all who could be affected by their actions.

Here follows an example of this process.

> Health economists and psychologists have considered how healthcare authorities could use their resources most beneficially for the well-being of all people affected by their policies – namely, the populations they serve. Since their aim was to help the authorities decide a policy on the use of resources for populations that may change over time, rather than deciding what to do in relation to particular individuals, they could not take account of the perspectives of particular people. Instead they have looked at information about what people in all cultures generally regard as important in having a life of good quality: the ability to perform certain functions, such as working, eating, being able to look after oneself, communicating with others, and so on. In the light of this information they have developed a unit of measurement known as a QALY (quality adjusted life-year). A life-year is one year of a person's life, and the quality of a life-year is measured by how well a person can perform these functions. The more someone can perform them – measured on a scale of, say, 1 to 10 – the higher a person's quality of life. By analysing the outcome of past uses of healthcare resources, calculations are made as to how many QALYs per unit cost (say £1000) each form of healthcare is likely to produce. This then gives a reasonably objective and impartial way of assessing which uses of resources – in this case, seen purely in financial terms – are likely to produce the best results for the well-being of the population served by the authority. The findings may be, for example, that the maximum benefits to the well-being of a population over the long term would be achieved by putting resources into educational and preventative health programmes (for instance, by educating people how to avoid disease, and by regular testing to detect early signs of disease) rather than by putting them into high-technology interventive medicine like heart/lung transplants. The latter are very expensive and prolong the quality life of only a few people, whereas the same amount of resources given to the former would increase by many years the quality life of hundreds of people. The QALY assessment not only makes clear the benefits that would be gained by allocating resources in this way, but also the benefits that would be lost by doing so – in this case, the benefit of interventive treatment to people who are currently in need

of it. In deciding which policy would be likely to lead to the best results for the population overall the health authorities must therefore weigh the benefits gained against those that would be lost by different uses of their resources.

By seeing the contribution to people's well-being simply as increases to their quality life-years, the economists and psychologists have a way of measuring and comparing benefits to different people and of judging which use of resources is likely to increase people's well-being by the greatest amount.

In many situations, however, it may not be possible to find units of measurement by which to measure and compare contributions to people's well-being. In these situations, professionals may sometimes find it helpful to think of people's well-being in terms of their preferences. Since 'preferences' is a neutral term, thinking in this way can enable them to take an appropriately neutral approach to the well-being of people who have a variety of values and cultural perspectives. According to this way of thinking, the obligation of professionals is to try to satisfy as many as possible of the preferences of the people who may be affected by their actions, while at the same time frustrating as few preferences as possible.

Taking account of people's preferences does not, however, mean enabling everyone always to have whatever they immediately want. This is illustrated by the following example.

> The policy committee of a regional social services organisation is considering whether to change its way of working (e.g. whether to go over to computerised records and data storage and adopt an automated telephone service for clients and members of the public). The purpose of doing so would be twofold: to free up more staff time by releasing personnel from basic telephone answering and other routine tasks; to make data available to staff more quickly.
>
> The changes would satisfy the long-term future preferences of staff to be released from certain tasks so they could do more productive and interesting work. On the other hand, learning how to operate the new systems would be an irksome and perhaps frustrating experience for them; so doing so would not be in accord with their immediate preferences. Similarly, initially at least, many clients and members of the public would prefer to speak to a person rather than a machine when making telephone contact, so the new system would frustrate at least their immediate, short-term preferences. On the other hand, once they had got used to it they might appreciate the greater speed with which they were put in contact with the appropriate person for

their particular enquiry, so the change might satisfy their future preferences.

The better informed the committee is about the preferences of its clients, staff and members of the public, the more responsibly it can make a decision based on the concern to achieve the best results for all. It might, therefore, be appropriate before making its decision to circulate a questionnaire explaining the reasons for, and the effects of, the changes, and asking for the views of those affected.

This example shows that trying to satisfy people's preferences involves working out how to meet as many of their current and likely long-term future preferences as possible. If we think their immediate preferences are likely to be short-lived, and their future preferences longer lasting, we may think we should give more importance to the latter, since this is likely to foster their well-being over the long term.

If professionals adopt this approach they should be mindful that an action likely to maximise the satisfaction of one person's preferences might frustrate those of someone else: one patient's preference to watch television all day might frustrate his neighbour's preference for silence. In these cases they must weigh the preferences of different people against each other and try to come up with a way forward that will satisfy as many, and frustrate as few, preferences as possible.

After taking account of everyone's preferences in this way, professionals must make their own judgements as to what course of action would be most likely to promote everyone's well-being as much as possible over the long term.

Assessing probabilities

When making such judgements professionals have to consider the probability of various consequences. To do this responsibly they must:

- be as well informed as they can be about their present situation and about the outcome of any previous similar situations

- try to anticipate factors that are not yet present but that might intervene.

Unfortunately, however well they are able to do this, they will usually have to accept a degree of uncertainty about what will actually happen, and this uncertainty is likely to be greater the further they look into the future. Given this uncertainty, and provided professionals have done all they can to foresee the likely consequences of alternative actions, they do not fail in their obligation to seek the best results if, when they act, the results are not as they had anticipated. People cannot be regarded as having an obligation to foresee more than is possible in their circumstances.

> Janet, a child protection officer, has to decide about taking a child into care. She is uncertain whether to remove seven-year-old Stephen from his family, where he is being physically and probably sexually abused by his drunken father, and exploited by his older siblings. He has a caring mother who is powerless to prevent the abuse, but she has a loving relationship with Stephen. Janet decides to remove him from his family. When she visits the family a few months later, the father's bouts of drunken violence have increased and Stephen seems happily settled in his new surroundings. Two years later, however, Stephen is very unhappy, and Janet realises that during the last year he has been abused in the residential home. Moreover he has had to suffer this ill-treatment without the loving support of his mother.

At the time Janet made her decision she made a careful assessment of likely outcomes. These indicated that better consequences would follow from removing Stephen from home than leaving him there. Janet could not reasonably have been expected to anticipate his abuse in the care home, so even though she was mistaken in her assessment of its outcome, she should not be morally blamed for this, nor should she blame herself. (For further discussion of blame see Chapter 11.)

Setting up rules of thumb for seeking the best results

So far we have considered the demands of the obligation to seek the best results on a case-by-case basis (i.e. by assessing the likely consequences of available options in each situation as it occurs).

Often no other way is possible: only by taking into account the complexities and details of a particular situation can professionals make an informed assessment of the probabilities of different consequences and their likely effects on everyone involved. The judgement as to what they ought to do to seek the best results follows from assessments based on the particular combination of factors in that situation. This means that if the same combination of factors were ever present on another occasion, those factors would give a reason for acting in the same way on that occasion also. So, once professionals are satisfied as to what they should do to seek the best results in a particular situation, they can use that as a guideline for relevantly similar situations in the future. They can set up 'rules of thumb' of the form 'In situations of type X, to seek the best results, do Y.'

These are, however, only rules of thumb – that is, rules to follow so long as there are no ethically relevant reasons not to do so. They are not absolute rules – that is, rules that must be followed come what may. Rules of thumb are useful guides when there is little time to think out what to do from scratch, but they allow for discretion not to follow them if good reasons subsequently emerge for not doing so. These reasons may be, for example:

- a future situation may not only have the same combination of factors but additional, previously unanticipated factors that affect the reliability of the calculations on which the rule of thumb is based

- events subsequent to setting up the rule of thumb suggest it should be modified (e.g. if the consequences expected from following the rule occurred on only a few occasions)

- ideas in the profession have changed and the grounds on which some results were thought preferable to others when setting up the rule of thumb are no longer held (e.g. giving a particular type of treatment to people with certain medical conditions is now no longer thought to lead to better results than other treatments).

Of course, such rules of thumb that are adopted are only guides as to what professionals should do in order to seek the best results. They do not take into account obligations that may arise from their other ethical principles: to act fairly, to act with integrity and to respect autonomy. These obligations may conflict with what should be done to seek the best results.

Ethical obligations that can conflict with seeking the best results

In order to consider some of the obligations that can conflict with seeking the best results we return to the QALY example.

In this example, once the professionals responsible for allocating the healthcare authorities' resources have assessed the likely effects of alternative policies, they must weigh the likely benefits and harms of the policies against each other. At that point, if their only ethical principle were to seek the best results, they would be obliged to carry out whichever policy would maximise the number of quality life-years, regardless of who would benefit and who would lose out. So if the greatest number of QALYs would result from using all their resources for the education of those who are currently well, then that is what they should do.

However, as professionals they must also be concerned to treat people fairly, to act with integrity and to respect autonomy. As we shall see in Chapter 6, part of what is involved in treating people fairly is to treat them as they are entitled to be treated and, since members of the population who are currently ill are entitled to receive the healthcare they need, it would be unfair on them if the health authorities ignored their entitlement in order to benefit others who are not yet ill. Moreover, as we shall see in Chapter 8, since the obligation of professionals to act with integrity requires them to provide services they have a professional remit, and are expected, to provide, the health authorities have a further ethical reason to meet the needs of those who are currently ill.

To fulfil their ethical responsibility, then, the authorities should reach their decision only after considering whether their ethical obligations conflict and, if they think they do, either seek a compromise between them or give priority to some over others. (In Chapter 9 we consider a compromise the authorities might arrive at.) In order to simplify the discussion of the authorities' situation we have assumed they have no legal obligations. If they had, then these would, of course, have to be given priority if they conflicted with the ethical concerns outlined.

In this example the authorities have to consider conflicting obligations to the currently well and the currently ill, both of whom are their 'clients', since both are part of the population they serve. However, in other situations, professionals may see a conflict between their obligations to those who are their clients and to those who are not. They may, for instance, consider that what will benefit their client will harm others. If they also think that the benefits to the client will be outweighed by the harm to others, then, from the point of view of the obligation to pursue the best results for all who may be affected by their actions, they should not pursue their client's well-being. However, as this is not their only ethical obligation, they must balance its importance against the importance of their other obligations. In Chapter 8 we look at an example of a situation where professionals must balance their ethical obligation to pursue the best results overall against their obligation to act in the best interests of their clients. In that chapter we see that acting in the best interests of clients is required by the principle to act with integrity. After considering the ethical demands of integrity, we look there at the issues to be considered when weighing the two obligations against each other. If you wish to consider them now, turn to p.144.

Before that, in Chapters 5 to 7, we look at situations in which seeking the best results conflicts with respecting clients' autonomy, with treating people fairly, and with fulfilling other professional commitments.

Seeking the best results does not, however, always conflict with other ethical obligations. In many situations the way for professionals to seek the best results is by acting with integrity, respecting autonomy and treating people fairly. That way they are likely to be trusted and able to achieve the professional objectives that contribute to the overall well-being of people affected by their work.

Questions

Promoting people's well-being:

1. Are there decisions about allocating resources that you or members of your profession find difficult to resolve?

2. Is the concern to bring about the best results the only ethical consideration you see as relevant to decisions about resources?

3. Do you think it sensible in your profession to see the best results in terms of promoting people's well-being?

4. Are there other elements in what you consider would be the best results for members of your profession to seek?

5. Are there important aspects of people's well-being that are omitted from the discussion in this section?

6. Would it be useful in any of the professional decisions you make to see 'benefit' in terms of satisfying people's preferences, and 'harm' in terms of going against their preferences?

7. Are there circumstances in which it would not be useful to think of results in terms of people's preferences?

8. Can you think of situations in your profession where the benefit of actions to promote the well-being of clients might be outweighed by the harm they would cause to others?

9. Are there individuals or groups of people with whom you work whose values and perspectives you find difficult to understand?

10. Are there some individuals or groups you find it more difficult to give full professional attention to than others? If so, why is this?

11. Are there any factors that make it difficult for you to have equal professional concern for the interests of all people you work with?

12. In your profession are there agreed ways of assessing the outcome of alternative procedures or ways of deploying resources?

13. Do you think it is possible to find reasonably objective ways of calculating and evaluating the benefits and harm of aspects of your work?

Setting up rules of thumb:

14. Does your profession have codes of conduct, protocols, and so on, that function as rules of thumb?

15. Can you think of consequential rules of thumb that might be adopted in your own profession?

16. Can you think of situations where you might think it appropriate not to follow a consequential rule of thumb? What would be your ethical reasons for not doing so?

17. Does your profession provide guidance on any of the issues raised in this chapter?

18. If you had problems in your work that relate to the issues raised in this chapter are there formal or informal opportunities to seek advice or discuss them with colleagues?

General issue:

19. Are there any legal or professional requirements on members of your profession that are relevant to the issues in this chapter?

Chapter 5

Treating People Justly and Fairly 1
The Principle of Justice and the Fairness of Compensating Disadvantages

Having looked in the last chapter at the principle to seek the best results, in this and the next we look at the principle to treat people justly and fairly. In Chapter 3 we summarised this as not discriminating between individuals on irrelevant grounds, and giving attention to their individual needs. In this chapter we consider what is meant by justice as fairness, and look at issues that arise when professionals consider whether they should compensate people who have been disadvantaged and, if so, how to do it justly and fairly. Chapter 6 looks at how professionals may justly and fairly take into account what people deserve and their needs, capacities and entitlement.

The principle of justice as fairness

The word 'justice' has at least two different meanings. First, it is used to mean the 'due process of law', or the correct operation of rules and disciplinary procedures of a particular profession or institution. So when people say they 'seek justice', or want to 'see justice done', they mean they want legal or disciplinary systems to operate correctly and to be seen to do so.

The other meaning of 'justice' refers to the general idea of treating people justly and fairly. We are here concerned with justice in this sense. Much of the work of professionals is concerned with providing 'benefits' (e.g. social welfare, police protection, legal representation, environmental protection, education, healthcare, counselling, professional expertise, jobs and career opportunities) and with distributing 'burdens' (e.g. exclusion from social welfare and other benefits of professional services, allocation to colleagues of extra responsibilities or unsocial working hours, deciding appropriate disciplinary action and punishment). In this and the next chapter we are concerned with their obligation to allocate these justly and fairly.

There are different ideological views on how benefits and burdens should be distributed justly. At the 'left-wing' end of the ideological spectrum is the socialist egalitarian view that it is just to distribute them so as to give people equal wealth, power, quality of life, and so on. At the 'right-wing' end of the spectrum is the view that it is just that people should have the freedom to retain, enjoy and dispose of whatever wealth, power and quality of life they have legally gained, and it is unjust to prevent this. The left sees injustice in inequality, the right in interfering with individual freedom. The left also tends to see justice as forward looking, as a means of bringing about equality by attending to people's needs. The right tends to see justice as backward looking, as a means of ensuring people are given what they are entitled to and what they deserve because of what they have done.

This chapter is not concerned with such ideological views. While they are often part of the political life of democracies, it is not part of the role of professions in such societies to espouse political views. They should only espouse those values – concern for results, fairness, integrity and respect for autonomy – that are broadly compatible with all political views that respect the basic elements of democracy (i.e. governments being democratically elected and individuals being held equal before the law).[1]

Although the notion of justice with which this chapter is concerned adopts neither a left nor a right perspective, it incorporates elements of each by taking the view that to treat people justly and fairly we should consider both their needs and what they deserve. In this way the notion aims to express a view of what it is to treat people justly and fairly that is as ideologically neutral as possible.

One of the neatest ways of expressing the kernel of this notion of justice as fairness is given by P.A. Facione, T. Attig and D. Scherer in their book *Values and Society* (1978, p.172) where they say:

> The basic principle underlying this sense of justice has come to be called the 'formal principle of justice'. It requires that persons who are alike in morally relevant respects be treated alike, and that persons who differ in morally relevant respects be treated differently in proportion to the differences between them.

As this quotation makes clear, to treat people justly and fairly, we must first consider whether there are any differences between them that are *morally relevant* to the situation we are concerned with. If there aren't any we should treat them alike, but if there are some we should treat them in ways that are appropriate to the differences between them. For example:

> A teacher taking reading classes with a new group of children first assesses whether there are any differences in their reading abilities and then treats them differently on this basis – giving the less advanced children different tasks from the more advanced. It would be unfair of her to treat all the children alike: the more advanced would get bored and the less advanced stressed. It would also be unfair for her to treat the children differently on the basis of a difference that is not relevant to the purpose of the reading class (e.g. by giving more attention to boys than girls).

Sometimes people assume that treating people fairly means treating everyone alike, but as the above example makes clear it is fair to treat individuals alike only when they are alike in morally relevant respects. If they are different in relevant respects it is wrong to treat them alike.

Fairness also requires us to be consistent in the way we take relevant differences into account: a teacher should give all pupils with the same reading ability tasks of equal difficulty (unless, of course, another relevant difference justifies her in doing otherwise).

Although people often use 'fairly' and 'justly' interchangeably, the two terms can be used to emphasise different aspects of justice: 'fairly' is more concerned than 'justly' with *comparing* the way individuals are treated, whereas 'justly' is more concerned than 'fairly' with making the treatment '*fitting*' for each individual.

Fairness emphasises the need to consider whether people are treated appropriately in comparison with others – that is, whether there really are differences between them that are relevant and so justify treating them differently.

> A police force recently adopted the policy of not following up burglaries where property of less than a certain value was taken. The idea was that officers' time could be used to bring greater benefit to the community in other ways. The policy was criticised as being unfair to some of the victims of burglary, because the difference between them – that some had been robbed of items of less value than others – was not relevant to the obligation to provide them with police services and

so did not justify treating them differently. Since all were entitled to these services, all should receive them.

'Justly' is concerned with treating people in ways that are appropriate, or 'fitting', for each of them, so it focuses on such questions as:

- What is the appropriate way to treat this person, given her needs and capacities, and so on?

- What must we do to ensure this person is sufficiently rewarded for the contribution she has made?

- What would be a just reward for this person?

- What punishment would be proportionate to what she has done?

Sometimes the distinction between these two aspects of justice is clear:

> Fifty students want to take a final-year undergraduate course but, because of limited resources, there are places for only 20 students. All 50 have good claims for being accepted on to the course: some have looked forward to taking it since they began their degree; some want to do it because it is relevant to their future careers; some have developed abilities that will enable them to do very well on the course. The staff cannot decide the basis on which to prioritise these competing claims, so put the names of all the students into a hat. The first 20 students whose names are drawn at random out of the hat go on the course. The staff see this as a *fair* procedure, since all students are treated alike in that all are subject to the same random chance of getting a place on the course. However, while students accept the process as fair in this general respect, they consider it has treated them *unjustly* as individuals, but for different reasons. Some think that those who had wanted to do the course for a long time should have been given preferential treatment; others felt that those for whom the course was relevant to their careers should have been given priority; still others felt that those whose abilities would have been able to shine on the course should have been given a place. So while they see the selection process as fair, they consider it has resulted in some of them being treated unjustly.

Much of the time, however, the difference between 'fairly' and 'justly' is not as apparent as it is in this situation. While it is sometimes helpful to distinguish them, as in this example, it is often difficult to separate the considerations each entails and so in this chapter we do not try to maintain a rigorous distinction between them.

Identifying differences that – from the point of view of justice and fairness – justify treating people differently

To be fair we should treat people differently only if differences between them are *relevant* to our treatment of them. But which differences are relevant?

In many cultures it has traditionally been thought appropriate to treat people differently if they are different in sex, tribal membership, culture, race or religion. In recent decades, however, people have increasingly questioned whether such general differences are really relevant to many situations. For example:

> Training for certain types of police duty – such as crowd control – has been offered by a police force only to its male officers. When this policy is challenged the justification given is that the work requires a certain level of strength and, since males are generally physically stronger than females, only men are considered appropriate for the work. Once it is acknowledged that physical strength and not gender is the relevant difference the male-only policy is agreed to be unfair and subsequently dropped.
>
> Similarly, only female officers are allowed to take training for bereavement duties because it is assumed that male officers would not be as sensitive as female officers in dealing with people who have been bereaved. This policy is dropped once it is clear that sensitivity rather than being female is the attribute most relevant to the work.

These cases show that to treat individuals justly we must identify *as precisely as possible* the differences between them that are relevant to a situation. We should then take into account only these factors when we are deciding how to treat people. If we do not do this we are in danger of discriminating unfairly against individuals because they are members of a particular group – for instance, because they are men or women – even though membership of this group is irrelevant to the situation.

These cases illustrate the dangers of stereotyping people and situations. We stereotype people when we assume that all members of a particular group have the same qualities, attributes or attitudes (e.g. all males are emotionally less sensitive than females). We stereotype situations when we regard them as appropriate only for members of particular groups, when, in fact, they may be just as appropriate for other people (e.g. when we regard jobs such as childcare as 'women's work' and others, such as lorry driving, as 'men's work').

Since the mid-twentieth century people have questioned whether it is *ever* ethically acceptable to treat people differently simply on grounds of general differences such as sex, age, race and sexual orientation. Article 2 of the United Nations Declaration of Human Rights 1948 states that everyone has the right to be treated without discrimination on grounds 'such as race, colour, sex, language, political or other opinion, national or social origin, property, birth or other status'; many professional codes contain similar assertions.

The perceived injustice of discriminating between individuals on these grounds has led many countries to adopt anti-discrimination and equal opportunities legislation. Where it is in force, all professionals must comply with this legislation, and many professions have policies and precise procedures that try to ensure that people are not treated differently simply because of differences in their sex, race, disability, age, sexual orientation or religion.

However, some people maintain that sometimes we *should* consider treating people differently if they have these differences. They consider, for example, that because some groups, such as women, members of ethnic and cultural minorities and people with disabilities, have been disadvantaged in the past, and may still be being disadvantaged, it is just to treat them differently from members of groups which have not been disadvantaged. We should do this by compensating them – by, for example, allowing members of a disadvantaged group to progress through an educational programme with qualifications which are lower than, or different from, the qualifications required of other groups. The argument for doing this is not that people should be treated differently simply because of their sex, race or disability but because they have been *disadvantaged* because of these factors.

Compensating people by positive discrimination in employment – for example, by giving higher or lower priority to applicants for a job because they are of a particular race, culture or gender, etc. – is normally illegal in many countries. However, insofar as there are legal ways of compensating groups of people for having been disadvantaged, some people maintain that they should be considered.

In the following two sections this view is discussed extensively to show the sort of analysis which may be necessary when professionals are considering whether a policy is ethically appropriate. If you do not wish to consider this matter at length, note the text in shaded boxes and move on to p.79.

Taking into account differences in the advantages and disadvantages that people experience

Many people consider that organisations and professions have an obligation to compensate people who have been disadvantaged by the society in which they operate. So, for example, professions in the United States should compensate black people for the fact that their ancestors were held in slavery, and professions in other countries should compensate women and members of cultural and racial minorities if they have been discriminated against in the past. One way of doing this is to give priority to the interests of all members of disadvantaged groups; another way is to give priority only to members who have themselves been disadvantaged. Such policies can take stronger or weaker forms. For example:

- strong positive discrimination gives higher priority to disadvantaged groups or individuals even when they are less qualified than other people

- weak positive discrimination gives higher priority to disadvantaged groups or individuals only when they are equally qualified with other people.

When thinking about the ethics of compensating disadvantages there are two main questions to consider.

1. Should compensation be carried out on a group or individual basis?

2. Is it fair and just to compensate people only for disadvantages that are the result of social forces – such as poverty or racial discrimination – or should people be compensated for disadvantages that are the result of other factors also – such as illness and disability?

In relation to the first question it is sometimes argued that it is fair and just to compensate all members of groups whose forebears have been disadvantaged because it:

- justly amends people for injustices against previous members of their group

- compensates groups whose members may still be disadvantaged, either by the legacy of past injustices or as a result of current discriminatory practices

- removes the advantages that current members of other groups (e.g. majority cultures or men) have acquired as a result of injustices their group has perpetrated.

There are, however, considerations which indicate that compensating people on a group basis for discrimination against members of their group is likely to lead to more injustice and unfairness than compensating only individuals who have themselves been disadvantaged. These considerations are as follows.

- The claim that compensation makes just amends for past injustices to people's forebears is questionable, since it is impossible to compensate the actual victims of those injustices (e.g. we cannot compensate the individuals who were actually taken as slaves or treated as the property of their husbands).

- The fact that the forebears of some people were discriminated against, and the forebears of others were not, is not a difference between them that is relevant to many current situations, whereas the fact that some individuals are currently disadvantaged *is* relevant.

- Compensation on a group basis will result in treating some individuals unjustly because:

  ○ it will inevitably give preferential treatment to some members of a group whose forebears, or who themselves, have not been disadvantaged, and so give them unfair and unjustified advantages

  ○ it makes higher demands of all members of other groups, irrespective of whether or not the individuals affected, or their ancestors, were responsible for the unfair treatment of members of the disadvantaged group; so it perpetrates another form of unfair group discrimination

  ○ some members of groups (e.g. poor members of racial or cultural majorities), whose forebears carried out injustices, have obviously not themselves been advantaged by them; consequently the fact that an individual is a member of an ethnic or cultural majority does not *in itself* justify making higher demands of him or her

- ◦ even if higher demands are made only of individual members of groups whose forebears are known to have committed injustices and who are clearly advantaged by the legacy of these injustices, these individuals are still being penalised unjustly since they are not responsible for the actions of their forebears; it would, therefore, be fairer to make higher demands only of individuals who have themselves unjustly disadvantaged others.

These considerations suggest that *in most situations* it is likely to be fairer and more just to make:

- lower demands only of individuals who have themselves been disadvantaged by social forces, rather than to all members of particular groups that have historically been disadvantaged
- higher demands only of those individuals who have themselves gained advantage by unfairly discriminating against others, rather than of all members of groups that have historically discriminated against others.

Of course, from the *consequential* perspective of seeking the best results, there could be considerations that support compensating people on a group basis. For example, members of races or cultures that have traditionally been discriminated against are often regarded as inferior to members of other groups, and so unworthy of equal respect. This is harmful both to them and society at large. If policies of group compensation were to:

- erode this view
- enhance opportunities for those who are seen as inferior to operate at higher levels
- enable communities and professions to benefit from having a greater diversity of people and cultures contributing at higher levels,

then these benefits may be thought to outweigh any injustices. However, when thinking of the likely effects of such policies, consideration must also be given to any harm they might cause. For example:

- the beneficiaries of compensation may be regarded as incapable
  of achieving much by their own abilities, so any status they gain
  by it may not in fact enhance the respect they receive from
  others

- if some people are thought to have received favourable
  treatment, and to have made gains other than by their own
  efforts, this may lead to social disharmony.

Consequently, where there are legally permissible ways of compensating people on a group basis for disadvantages, these should be considered only if there is clear evidence that their benefits would outweigh any harm and injustices they may cause.

Is it fair to compensate people for disadvantages other than those arising from social forces?

As we have seen, fairness requires us to treat people alike unless there are relevant differences between them. This being so, if we are to compensate individuals who have been disadvantaged in some ways, we should compensate those who have been disadvantaged in others, as long as these disadvantages are relevant to our situation.

Disadvantages other than those resulting from social forces are in fact often considered relevant to situations involving professionals. For example:

> If a young offender has been disadvantaged because he has been physically abused by his father or rejected by his mother, a court of law may consider it just to give him a less severe punishment than if he had not been treated badly by his parents.

> University examination boards often consider it just to give 'the benefit of the doubt' to (i.e. compensate) students who have been disadvantaged by 'mitigating circumstances' – such as illness or bereavement – which may have adversely affected their performance. Compensation may take the form of crediting the students with a pass even though their marks indicate a narrow failure.

A policy to compensate only those disadvantages that arise from social forces requires people to identify and categorise the causes of people's problems. This is often not easy. For example, even if it is known that someone's education has been impaired by parental poverty, it may be difficult to ascertain whether this is because her family is part of a group discriminated against by society, or because her father was treated badly by his employer, or because he had long periods of illness, or because he was lazy, or for a mixture of such reasons. Since most professions and organisations do not have enough knowledge of individuals' lives to judge the extent to which their disadvantages are socially induced, injustices can occur if they set out to compensate only those that are. Consequently, *from the perspective of justice and fairness*, it is questionable whether professions and organisations should have policies to compensate socially induced disadvantages only.

Of course, from the consequential perspective, it might be argued, as previously, that concerns about these injustices should be overridden, if they are likely to be outweighed by the benefits of such policies. However, people can make judgements about this only if they have sufficient knowledge to assess and compare policies that compensate only socially induced disadvantages with ones that compensate other disadvantages also. This evidence may be difficult to obtain. On the face of it, however, it would seem that if policies of compensation generally bring benefits, they are likely to produce more benefits the more types of disadvantage they compensate.

If legally permitted policies of compensation are considered justified, there are strong grounds of both fairness and consequences for compensating all relevant disadvantages, and not just those caused by social forces.

Implications for professional practice

This chapter indicates that when professionals consider how to treat people fairly and justly they should bear in mind the following points.

Fairness requires us to treat the interests of all people as equally important

It is not always easy to treat the interests of everyone as equally important. In all societies some groups have more power than others, and some are conventionally regarded as superior to others. As a result we are all subject to social and psychological influences that can cause us to see the interests of some people as more important than the interests of others. Since it is difficult to eradicate these influences, it may be impossible for professional people to rid themselves completely of such attitudes. But whatever may be in their hearts and minds, in their professional activities they should treat the interests of all people they are working with as equally important, regardless of their 'group membership'. They should give different priorities to the interests of some people over others only when there are differences between them that are relevant to the professional situation and that justify so doing.

It is normally unfair to treat people differently solely on grounds of general differences

It is unjust and unfair on individuals to regard general differences such as race, gender and disability as differences that in themselves justify treating people differently, unless these differences are demonstrably relevant to a situation.

There is a need to avoid stereotyping

Professionals should be wary of stereotyping people not only by race, sex, age and cultural affiliation, but also by physical appearance and behavioural factors. They should ask themselves such questions as:

- Do I, consciously or unconsciously, regard all people in a particular category as having the same characteristics (e.g. do I think of all thin people as neurotic, all fat people as lazy, all tall people as dynamic/authoritative, all short/red-haired people as aggressive)?

- Do I regard people with particular regional accents as unintelligent/trustworthy (e.g. 'People with Scottish accents are honest and straightforward')?

- Do I assume all people with certain class accents have particular attitudes (e.g. 'People with upper-class accents are unsympathetic to the plight of others', 'People who have regional accents are less well informed than those who don't')?

Although most professionals may consider they are too sophisticated to think in these ways, from time to time such attitudes emerge in discussions between professionals – especially when they are finding it difficult to work with particular colleagues, clients or members of the public.

There is a need to identify as precisely as possible the differences between individuals that are relevant to a situation

When concerned to identify differences that may justify giving priority to some individuals over others, it is sometimes useful to adopt the criterion of 'practical necessity' – for instance:

- What abilities and skills must individuals have to be successful in this job or to achieve the objectives of the project in hand (e.g. physical strength, sympathetic manner)?

- What attributes must someone have to need this service (e.g. what medical condition a patient should have, what abilities a student should have)?

There is a need to avoid actions that unintentionally disadvantage others

Professionals should be aware of ways in which they can unintentionally disadvantage colleagues, clients and members of the public. For example:

- reliance on 'old boy/old girl' networks

- failure to ensure that what they communicate, either in speech or writing, is understood by everyone, with the result that lay people, or those from certain cultural backgrounds, cannot understand what is meant

- vocabulary and body language that reveal discriminatory attitudes

- failure to provide ease of access for physically disabled people

- devising curricula and training programmes that are more accessible to some people than others

- using examples to illustrate points that are outside the experience of some people.

While professionals should make every effort not to discriminate against people unintentionally, it is unjust to regard unintentional discrimination as equally reprehensible as intentional discrimination. It is also often counter-productive to do so: it can make the people who are trying to avoid discrimination feel their efforts are unappreciated.

There is a need to consider whether, if legal, professionals have an obligation to compensate people for having been disadvantaged

Professionals should consider the following questions.

1. Do members of this profession have an ethical obligation to try to compensate people who are disadvantaged as a result of factors outside the profession?

2. Do they have an ethical obligation to compensate people who have been unjustly disadvantaged by the profession itself?

3. Do they have an ethical obligation to ensure they do not, now or in the future, unjustly disadvantage people either by their general practices or by ad hoc decisions?

While it may be debatable whether members of a profession have the first obligation, it is usually considered that they have the second and third.

POINTS RELATING TO QUESTION 1

When answering this question, professionals should be mindful of the key points made on pp.75–79. They should also consider:

-   which disadvantages caused by factors external to their profession are relevant to their professional situations and so might be appropriately compensated by them

-   which disadvantages they are able to compensate in their professional activities

-   whether members of their profession are likely to have sufficient information to ascertain accurately the extent to which individuals have been disadvantaged by factors external to their profession.

The importance of good information when professionals are trying to compensate people for disadvantages caused by external factors is evident in the arrangements of examination boards to compensate candidates for such misfortunes as illness and bereavement. In order to do this fairly these boards have procedures to ensure that:

-   all candidates know how to submit information to the board

-   corroborative evidence is available as far as possible

-   information is communicated to the board in a consistent manner

-   the board applies agreed and known criteria uniformly.

Professionals should be wary of compensating disadvantages caused by factors external to their profession unless they are likely to have sufficient knowledge of the circumstances of everyone involved to:

- assess any injustices that may be caused by doing so
- assess the likely benefits and harms of doing so.

POINTS RELATING TO QUESTION 2

The case on grounds of justice and fairness for members of a profession to compensate people for disadvantages their profession has unjustly caused is stronger than that for compensating disadvantages that are externally induced.

Professionals can sometimes be considered to have disadvantaged someone through the normal pursuit of their professional objectives – for example, in fighting for the interests of her client, a lawyer may disadvantage the interests of her client's adversary. However, so long as this is done legitimately and within normal professional practice such disadvantaging cannot be regarded as unjust. Unjust disadvantaging occurs when professionals, inadvertently or not, disadvantage someone for no acceptable professional reason (e.g. a professional omits to inform a client of a deadline to be met and the client's interests suffer as a result). It is clearly just that professions should compensate those they have disadvantaged in such ways.

Any ethical reasons against doing so are likely to be less powerful than those against compensating people for externally caused disadvantages. Accurate knowledge of professionally induced disadvantages is likely to be greater than for those caused by factors external to the profession, so the chances of treating people unfairly – say by compensating some but not all who are equally entitled – are likely to be less. Moreover, consequential considerations are more likely to support compensation in these cases. Knowledge of the outcome of previous cases is likely to be available and to show that benefits have accrued both to the people compensated and to the profession itself by it being seen to have made amends for wrongs it has committed. It may also be more obvious how a profession can provide appropriate compensation for disadvantages it has unjustly caused than for disadvantages caused by external factors. Indeed, fair and just formulae for doing so may be part of established procedures.

On grounds of both fairness and of seeking the best results, members of professions have an ethical obligation to compensate people who have been unjustly disadvantaged by their profession.

POINTS RELATING TO QUESTION 3

Considerations of justice and fairness give professionals an obvious obligation to ensure they do not unjustly disadvantage individuals by their current
procedures and practices. Moreover, consequential considerations are likely
be in agreement with this, since normally it is to the benefit of:

- individuals not to be disadvantaged

- a profession not to be seen to act unjustly

- a community to have professions that achieve their socially
  valuable objectives in ways that do not damage the trust placed
  in them.

This chapter has looked at what is meant by justice as fairness, and at the
extent to which members of professions can justly and fairly compensate
people in relation to their disadvantages. Chapter 6 considers the extent to
which professionals can justly and fairly take into account what people
deserve and their needs, capacities and entitlement.

Questions

1. Is there a tendency among members of your profession to regard
   the interests of some people for whom you work as more
   important than the interests of others?

2. Are there practices in your profession that unjustly stereotype
   people or situations?

3. Do you stereotype people in any way?

4. Are there ways in which your profession unjustly disadvantages
   some people? If so, what steps can be taken to avoid this in the
   future?

5. Do you think members of your profession have an ethical
   obligation to compensate people unjustly disadvantaged by your
   profession?

6. If so, how do they, or should they, do this?

7. In what ways may the people for whom you work have been
   disadvantaged by factors external to your profession (e.g.
   poverty, illness)?

8. Which of these disadvantages are relevant to the work of your professions?

9. Do you think members of your profession have an ethical obligation to compensate people for having been disadvantaged by such factors, if they can do so legally?

10. If so which sort of factors should it:

    • strive to compensate

    • not strive to compensate?

    What are your reasons for rejecting some factors?

11. Does your profession already try to compensate people who have been disadvantaged by external factors (e.g. as in examination boards of universities where illness of candidates is taken into account)?

12. Are there other ways in which your profession could justly and fairly compensate disadvantaged people?

13. Does your profession provide guidance on issues to do with treating people fairly?

14. If you have problems in your work that relate to the issues raised in this chapter, are there formal or informal opportunities to seek advice or to discuss them with colleagues?

15. Are there any legal or professional requirements on members of your profession that are relevant to the issues in this chapter?

Note

1   There is arguably a further reason for professional values not to include extreme left- or right-wing ideological perspectives: they can be difficult to square with the balancing of ethical demands and the objectives of some professions. For example, arrangements necessary to achieve the radical left-wing aim of equality of wealth, power and quality of life would involve great restrictions on individual freedom and autonomy (people would not, for example, be able to earn, inherit or pay others above a certain amount) and it is questionable how far professionals in democratic societies could go along with that. Similarly, the right-wing view that individuals are entitled to enjoy all that they have legally gained implies that they should be free of taxation, which is the source of social welfare. But what, then, should be done about those – the sick, the orphans and the elderly – who are unable to provide for themselves and whose needs many professions have an obligation to try to meet?

Chapter 6

Treating People Justly and Fairly 2
Taking into Account What People Deserve and Their Entitlement, Needs and Capacities

In the last chapter we considered the extent to which professionals can justly and fairly take into account people's disadvantages. In this chapter we consider the extent to which they can justly and fairly take into account differences in what people deserve and are entitled to, and differences in their needs and capacities.

We are, of course, exploring here what is just and fair *ethically*: we are not exploring what is just and fair from a legal point of view. Professionals should ensure they are aware of any legal or professional requirements upon them in relation to the issues discussed here.

Taking into account differences in what individuals deserve

As we saw at the beginning of the last chapter an important aspect of treating individuals justly and fairly is treating them as they deserve. People are generally thought to deserve benefits and relief from burdens if they have 'earned' them in some way, the main ways being:

- by contributions they have made
- by efforts they have made to contribute
- by how responsibly they have behaved.

But what sort of contributions, efforts and responsible behaviour might professionals take into account when considering how people deserve to be treated, and how fair and just is it to use these as indications of what people deserve?

As the principle of justice as fairness set out at the beginning of the last chapter makes clear, people are only justified in treating others differently if the differences between them are relevant to the way they are to be treated. So differences in people's contributions, efforts and responsibility only justify professionals in treating them differently if they are relevant to the particular professional activity or service. But what counts as relevant? If someone puts a lot of effort into raising money for the hardship fund for retired police officers, does he deserve preferential treatment when unpopular duties are allocated?

Although professionals may consider a client's or colleague's contribution to activities other than the immediate work of their profession to be valuable and admirable, they should question whether that person should be regarded as more deserving of preferential treatment by their profession on that account. The views of individual professionals about the value of activities that do not contribute directly to achieving professional objectives may be influenced by ideological, religious or personal values which, as we have seen, are inappropriate in professional judgements. In addition, since it may be a matter of chance whether professionals know about such contributions, to take them into account could be unfair on the people about whom they know little. These problems are likely to be avoided if professionals consider as relevant only the contribution, effort and responsibility of individuals that *directly* promote the objectives of their profession. For example, if in addition to his normal duties a lecturer organises his department's timetable, this is a direct contribution to the work of his profession.

We now consider the main practical and ethical issues involved in taking the contributions of colleagues and clients in professional situations as an indication of what they deserve. We will later discuss effort and levels of responsibility.

Contributions as an indication of what individuals deserve

Many performance-related pay schemes are based on judging people's contributions in terms of what they produce that enables their work to achieve its objectives. In such schemes individuals' contributions are seen as their productivity in enabling specific targets to be reached. It is seen as just that the more they actually produce, the more they are paid.

Measuring the extent to which individuals contribute to the objectives of their work may be straightforward in some situations: for example, in an organisation set up to produce widgets individuals' contribution can be measured by counting the number of widgets they produce. However, it is rarely so straightforward in the professions, for several reasons.

First, many professionals work in fluid and complex situations where the variety of valuable – and sometimes alternative – outcomes makes it difficult to measure and compare their contributions to their profession's objectives. For example:

> Police officers patrol town streets late at night as drunken crowds leave pubs and clubs. The number of arrests an officer makes might seem a good indicator of his or her productivity, since someone who is arrested and removed from the streets cannot cause further crimes and breaches of the peace. However, an officer who is able to defuse tensions so that no crimes are committed and no arrests are necessary may contribute more to good policing than the officer who makes many arrests. But it is difficult to quantify an officer's contribution by trying to assess the crimes and disorder he may have prevented. It is also difficult to compare this with the number of arrests made by another officer.

> For mental health nurses working in a hospital the number of patients per nurse may seem a reasonable basis for measuring their productivity. However, it gives no indication of the quality of their care nor its results. Results – such as the long-term conditions of patients – often cannot be attributed to the care of particular nurses, and in any case quality of care may be difficult to assess in any objective way if patients are too ill to give reliable information as to how they are treated.

Second, it can be difficult to identify and measure the contribution of individuals to the objectives of their profession in situations where the objectives clash. For example, police officers should aim both to keep the peace and prevent crime, but in some situations they may find they can only prevent a minor crime by creating a major breach of the peace: an intervention to prevent a minor affray among demonstrators may inflame a whole crowd to go on the rampage. Similarly, healthcare professionals are expected to prolong life and give comfort to those who are terminally ill, but they sometimes cannot prolong a patient's life without causing discomfort and damage to his or her quality of life. In such situations the professional has to judge which objective to prioritise in the particular circumstances, and attempts to find measurable targets of productivity, or other specific criteria as to what shall count as a contribution, can make a mockery of such judgements.

Third, not only is it difficult to identify and measure the contributions of professionals in complex situations, it can also be difficult to *compare* their contributions to different situations. Even if a way of measuring the contributions of officers on patrol on Saturday nights could be established, how do we compare that with the contribution of police officers visiting schools to promote children's safety on the roads?

Given these difficulties, injustices can arise in trying to measure and compare the contributions of professionals or of clients to the objectives of a profession.

In addition to these difficulties, there is the major issue of whether it is fair to base someone's 'deservingness' on what they actually manage to contribute, since what someone actually produces or contributes can be affected by factors beyond their control. It may, indeed, be a matter of luck. Someone may work hard but achieve little because, for instance, she has not been given the training her colleagues have had, or because her computer crashes, or because she teaches a minority-interest subject and her productivity – in terms of the numbers of students she teaches – can never be high. Conversely, some people may be in situations where they can be very productive with comparatively little effort – as when a lecturer of a popular subject assessable by computer can conduct courses with large numbers of students without much effort.

Matters of luck also affect the contributions to professional processes made by clients, patients, students, and so on. Lecturers are sometimes inclined to regard as more deserving of their attention those students they think have worked hard, and healthcare professionals sometimes regard patients who do everything to promote their own recovery as more deserving of help than those who do not. But how much or how little individual students or patients actually manage to do may be the result of many factors over which they have little control. This being so, it is unjust to regard what they actually contribute as a good indication of what they deserve in terms of services.

From these considerations it is clear that professionals need to be very well informed about the circumstances of colleagues and clients before they judge that their actual contribution to professional processes makes them more or less deserving of opportunities, support, attention and care.

Professionals should be wary of regarding colleagues' and clients' actual contributions to the work of their profession as an indicator – and certainly as the only indicator – of what they deserve. They should consider doing so only if they have clear criteria, known and preferably agreed by members of the profession (and clients if appropriate) on how their contributions should be identified and assessed. Generally, the more other indicators of what people deserve can be taken into account, the better.

Effort as an indication of what people deserve

An alternative – or additional – indicator of what people deserve is the effort they make towards the work of a profession. 'Effort', more than 'productivity' and 'contribution', suggests something that is relative to a particular person in particular circumstances. 'Effort' invites consideration of what can be expected in a specific situation of a colleague or client with a particular background, ability and training, and who may be affected by favourable or unfavourable factors over which they have no control. Consequently, in many situations, assessing effort may well be fairer than trying to quantify contributions or productivity.

However, to do so can involve complex judgements. Even when looking at simple tasks it may be necessary to think of both the time and ingenuity someone puts into them. A colleague may spend long hours on a project and apparently be making much effort, but if he is not prepared to work out a quicker way of doing it he may be given credit for what is in fact a lazy way of working. On the other hand, he may not have the ability to work out a quicker way – which is why when effort is assessed the focus must be on what can be expected of someone with a particular education, social circumstances, ability and background. In more complicated situations other matters will also be relevant. For example:

- Does a colleague or client make the effort to draw on whatever professional expertise is available to her?

- Has she made the effort to be as well informed as she can be?

- Has she thought through the issues as much as she can in the time available?

- Has a client, student or patient made whatever arrangements he can to carry out his tasks properly?

- Has he used the resources available to help him?

It is obviously important that when professionals are assessing a colleague's or client's effort they should only do so on the basis of information that is as good as possible. It is also clear that, in the interests of justice and fairness, when someone's deservingness is judged their *effort* to contribute should be considered as well as – or instead of – their actual contribution to the work of the profession.

Responsibility and irresponsibility as an indication of what people deserve

The third factor many people regard as relevant when considering what people deserve is whether they have acted responsibly or irresponsibly, and whether their problems are 'their own fault'.

We often consider people whose deliberate actions have caused their own problems to be irresponsible and less deserving of help than those whose problems are caused by factors beyond their control. So a colleague who does not bother to read the guidance on how to carry out a procedure may be regarded as less deserving of help from co-workers than someone who does. Someone who knowingly and persistently takes risks to their health and safety may be considered less deserving of medical help than others – people may, for example, think that injured skydivers are less deserving of free medical treatment than victims of motor accidents, or that someone who continues to smoke after being treated for smoking-related illnesses should be given low priority for further treatment. Such a view is not, however, professional policy. Similarly, someone who is careless about the security of her home may be seen as less deserving of police help after a robbery than someone who has taken all reasonable precautions – though such a view is unlikely to be part of police policy.

The main problem with making judgements about whether people have acted irresponsibly is knowing whether their behaviour was, in fact, deliberate and intentional, or whether it was irresponsible negligence or the result of factors over which they had no control. While there may be little doubt that the skydiver acted deliberately, we may not be so certain about the smoker, who may find it impossible to give up. The person who failed to lock her front door may not have been irresponsibly negligent but so concerned with an urgent family matter she does not wish to disclose that, if it were known, her oversight might be thought excusable. And the colleague who failed to read the guidance may have been under time pressure because he has taken on extra work to help someone else.

As these examples suggest, when we have evidence about why people behaved as they did we may see them as only partially responsible for their problems. Comparing the extent to which we should hold people responsible for their problems can be difficult.

As we have previously observed, professionals cannot justly and fairly judge what people deserve unless they are well informed about their individual situations. This is particularly so when they attempt to judge how responsibly others have behaved. It is doubtful, therefore, whether it is ever fair for them to use this as a basis for regarding some people as more or less deserving than others. (For a discussion of moral responsibility, see Chapter 11.)

When deciding how it is fair and just to treat people, professionals should not give greater importance to what they consider individuals deserve as a result of their contribution, effort and responsibility than is warranted by their knowledge of each person and their situation.

It is indeed questionable whether professionals should ever, on grounds of fairness, consider giving an individual higher or lower priority for their services because they consider that person more or less deserving than others because of factors discussed here.[1] Moreover, their professional codes of conduct may well prohibit them from doing so.

Taking into account differences in individuals' entitlement

If people are entitled to certain things, it is only fair that they should be given that to which they are entitled.

Individuals become entitled to the services of professionals by various means – by, for example, paying fees to them directly, by contributing to public or private insurance schemes, by entering into relationships with professionals on the understanding that services will be made available to them, and by being citizens to whom professionals have obligations. People may, for instance, be entitled to healthcare, education or police protection because they have paid towards an insurance scheme or taxes, or simply because they are citizens of a nation state.

Members of professions become entitled to benefits from their profession as a result of contracts, employment law, formal agreements and informal but reasonable expectations.

In so far as individuals have the same entitlements, the principle of fairness requires that they should be given the same level of service or other benefits, but if they have different entitlements that they be treated differently.

Whether or not individuals have particular entitlements is usually a factual matter. Once these facts are clear, the obligations of professionals to individuals on grounds of entitlement are usually also clear.

In many cases professions and their members will have legal obligations to meet people's entitlements. In other cases, these obligations will be ethical. When this is the case, professionals sometimes have to balance these obligations against others, since it does not follow from the fact that someone is entitled to professional services – such as healthcare or education – that a particular professional has the obligation to provide them when requested, if at all. There may be more urgent ethical demands on that professional's time and resources, including prior commitments to others who are similarly entitled. On the other hand, a profession will normally have a collective ethical obligation to provide the services within a reasonable time.

Taking into account differences in what individuals need

It is widely thought that to treat people fairly and justly we should take account of differences in their needs as well as differences in their entitlement. It is seen as *just* that those who have the greatest need should receive the greatest benefit or greatest relief from burdens. In other words, the benefits and relief from burdens given to individuals should be proportionate to their needs. Incidentally, the consequential concern for results is also likely to support this, since by giving the most to people with the greatest needs we may bring about the greatest happiness, or the greatest relief from suffering, possible with the resources at our disposal. But what types of benefit and relief from burden is it fair and just to give?

Benefits and reliefs should be relevant to people's needs: giving food to those who need it not only relieves their hunger but is just compensation for what they lack. Sometimes, however, when people are not able to give benefits that are relevant to someone's needs they give them other benefits as a gesture of goodwill. Though this may be a welcome impulse, is it fair to do it? Consider the following:

> A police officer has more children than his colleagues and desperately needs more money to buy a larger house. However, all officers on his grade receive a certain level of salary that cannot be varied according to their needs. Because his senior officer cannot give him the benefit he needs, she shows her concern by excusing him from stressful duties – such as attending road traffic accidents. But this is unfair on the other officers: they are given a larger share of stressful duties than they would otherwise receive and he gets none, even though his difference from them (i.e. his need for more money) is irrelevant to the allocation of these duties.

In this example the senior officer, out of goodwill to one officer, ends up treating the others unfairly. If we cannot meet people's needs, giving them unrelated benefits and relief from unrelated burdens may be unfair on others.

Of course there may be consequential reasons for giving unrelated benefits and reliefs – the officer in the above example may have been able to cope better with his overcrowded family because his work was less stressful. As ever, to decide whether the value of consequences would be likely to outweigh the unfairness of giving unrelated benefits, professionals must be well informed, not only about the circumstances of everyone involved but how they would all perceive the giving of such benefits.

To treat everyone fairly and justly, we should, of course, not only give benefits and relief from burdens that are proportionate and relevant to their needs, but should give them impartially and consistently. Those with similar needs should receive similar benefits, regardless of the greater sympathies we may have for some people than others.

Is it more fair to satisfy uniform or varying levels of need?

Since the totality of people's needs frequently exceeds the resources available to meet them, professionals may have to find just and fair criteria for selecting the needs to be met. There are two basic approaches to doing this. One is to identify a *uniform level* of essential need for everyone, and to give priority to meeting this level before providing for any needs above that level. The other is to identify *varying levels* of need that are regarded as essential for the welfare of different individuals, or of people in different cultures or groups. When all needs cannot be met, these varying essential needs should be met before any non-essential ones. Each approach has its merits and limitations. As we shall see, in some circumstances they can be complementary.

As already indicated, the uniform needs approach claims that it is just and fair to give priority to meeting the same level of need for everybody before meeting any needs above that level. Consequential considerations may also support this approach: it is reasonable to think that the greatest improvement in people's well-being and relief from misery will be achieved by satisfying a basic level of need for all before using resources for other purposes. The problem with this approach, however, is identifying a uniform level of need that is fair to everyone.

In situations of acute deprivation we may unchallengeably identify clean drinking water as at least one essential need. But fixing a uniform level of cleanliness is difficult, since one that would keep some people healthy would not be adequate for others. A uniform level might be unnecessarily high and wasteful of resources when applied to some people, while being less than satisfactory for others. It would then be unfair on those for which it was not high enough to refuse to make it higher, since their essential needs would not be given the same attention as the essential needs of others.

In situations of less acute deprivation (i.e. situations in which most professions operate) essential needs are often seen as what is necessary for people's physical and psychological health, such as adequate diet and accommodation, and the freedom to live in personal relationships of their choice. It is difficult to establish a uniform level of these needs that is fair to all, since the diet, accommodation and social arrangements that would maintain the physical and psychological health of people in some cultures would not do so in others. For example, people in some societies generally have more accommodation space per person than people in others, and it would be a psychological hardship for them to live at a level of crowding that would not cause problems to others. It is questionable, then, whether it is fair to try to meet a uniform level of need for people across all cultures and societies before meeting any needs above that level.

It is also questionable whether it is fair to work to a uniform level of need for everyone within a particular culture or society, since what some people would regard as essential to their physical and psychological health would be a luxury for others in the same society. Individuals' needs vary as a result of their temperament, upbringing, expectations, jobs and lifestyle. Some people need space in which to have time alone, but others do not; some find it a hardship not to have access to a flushing toilet or to their own kitchen, but others do not; and some need enough accommodation to have several members of their family living with them, but others do not.

Moreover, the uniform level of need approach can lead to the imposition of social arrangements on some people who do not want them, because they are necessary for the well-being of others. For example, because the freedom to choose one's spouse is essential to the psychological health of people in some cultures, some people consider it essential for people in all cultures. As a result there can be international pressure on some cultures to abolish all forms of arranged marriage. It could be argued, however, that it is unfair to urge people in these cultures to give up their social arrangements when others are not required to give up theirs.

In view of these problems, the varying level approach (i.e. seeing essential needs as relative to the welfare of particular cultures, groups or individuals) is worth considering as a way of treating people fairly. However, it too has its problems.

One problem is how to distinguish between needs that are *essential* to the well-being of a particular individual or group and what they merely *want*. And who should make the distinction? Individuals identifying their own needs may find it difficult to distinguish between their needs and wants, and it may seem unfair if some perceive their own needs as greater than those of others. On the other hand, if the needs of individuals are identified by other people – for example, by members of an agency or profession – they may not fully understand the individuals' values and lifestyles, and so include factors that are not essential to their well-being or exclude ones that are.

Another problem with the varying level approach is whether it is fair to attempt to meet people's needs that arise from their own choices. These needs may be for quite ordinary things, such as extra accommodation for couples who have chosen to have many children, or for rather esoteric things, such as ballet classes for someone who has chosen to be a dancer. Should needs that are basic to people's chosen lifestyles be met, whatever they are? If not, what is a fair way to decide which choices should have their needs met and which should not? Can needs arising from choices be separated from wants? And if it is decided not to provide for needs arising from choices how can we be sure that people's choices really have been made freely, and are not the result of circumstances beyond their control?

A combined approach

Because of the difficulties of finding fair and just ways of identifying and prioritising essential needs when taking only the uniform level or only the varying level view, in many professional situations the fairest approach may be to include both.

Professionals concerned with the provision of resources to people in general (e.g. housing, education, community facilities) might formulate normal uniform standards of essential need for all (it would be seen as fair and just for them to do this). However, they should then be prepared to vary the resources they provide relative to the needs of particular cultures or groups. The point of setting a normal standard is that any variations from it have to be justified. The onus is on those who wish to deviate from it to demonstrate that there are differences in people's essential needs that are relevant to the situation. For example, policies for community facilities might have normal standards for communities of a certain size but allow variations for populations with particular cultural priorities; so some may need more religious centres, others more sports halls.

Similarly, professionals who make decisions about resources for individuals (e.g. local housing officers, counsellors, teachers) might adopt the combined approach by setting up normal standards of essential need for people in particular types of situation, but then be prepared to vary what is allocated to satisfy the most important needs of particular individuals.

> A housing agency has normal standards of accommodation for everyone with three children, but officers vary what is provided for those with special needs, including those that arise from their cultural background. If they do vary the provision, they can account for the variations they judge appropriate.

When professions are dealing with the needs of their members, and professionals with the needs of their colleagues, they might also take the combined approach by setting up normal standards of need – say for parental leave – but be prepared to deviate from it if individuals unavoidably have greater needs.

When adopting this combined approach professionals should, of course, strive to be objective and impartial. To be as objective as possible, they should try to see the effects of meeting any variations in the normal standard from the perspectives of all the people affected. They should take account of how people with particular cultural and personal backgrounds, emotions and expectations are likely to feel. Ideally, deviations from the standard would be agreed only after discussion with all groups or individuals affected, and professionals would only accept that cultural or community factors justify deviations after their relevance to the situation has been accepted generally. People are then more likely to be treated justly and their needs met.

To be as impartial as possible, professionals should avoid favouritism. If, for example, they decide that benefits to the people with particular disadvantages should be greater than benefits to others, they should apply this policy impartially, giving more benefits to all those who are disadvantaged in this way. They might also consider making the total provision of facilities and services received by each group or individual – even though there are variations within them – roughly the same. So if some people have more of one facility they have less of another.

Taking people's needs into account by the combined approach may in many situations be the fairest, most just way for professionals to do so. It may also be the way to achieve the most valuable consequences.

Fair treatment of people with no pressing needs

Before leaving the issue of how professionals may justly and fairly take people's needs into account, there is one other matter to consider.

It is often thought fair to give people who have no pressing needs more burdens than to those who have obvious needs. Consider the following:

> In a class of 30 children, 10 have no learning problems and so no need for more than the normal amount of attention from the teacher. The teacher gives all the burdensome tasks to these children and none to those who are struggling with their studies. Whether this is fair depends upon whether the tasks would exacerbate the children's problems with their studies. If they would, it would not be fair not to give them the tasks. But if the tasks would not exacerbate their problems, then it is unfair to regard these problems as a reason for not giving them the tasks. From a consequential perspective, of course, there might be a reason to give the tasks to the children without problems since they might do them better than the others, and so all would benefit. Whether or not the benefits would be thought to outweigh the unfairness would, of course, depend on the circumstances.

If people – colleagues or clients – have no pressing needs it does not necessarily follow that it is fair to give them more burdens than others.

Taking into account differences in individuals' capacities

People have different capacities as well as different needs. By 'capacities' in this context is meant latent or actual abilities and interest in carrying out activities which are generally regarded as desirable or beneficial – such as caring for people, analysing problems and motivating others.

In many areas of life it is accepted that people who have more of certain capacities should receive more benefits: children with more academic intelligence than others have traditionally been given more educational resources and have expected to go into jobs commanding higher incomes. However, people with more capacities are often also expected to take on more burdens.

> Because of her leadership skills and capacity for administration a
> lecturer is asked to spend three years running a university department.
> It is not a job she particularly wishes to do, but she does it excellently.
> None of her colleagues has similar capacities so at the end of three
> years she comes under heavy pressure to continue.

There are often, of course, strong consequential reasons for concentrating
resources on people whose capacities are valuable, and for requiring them to
exercise them: doing so is likely to benefit others, and people often enjoy
exercising their capacities when they feel valued by their neighbours and
colleagues.

But while such practices may be justifiable from a consequential point of
view, are they fair and just? Fairness and justice require everyone to be given
equal opportunities to develop their capacities and to be under equal
pressure to use them, unless there are differences between the individuals
which justify treating them differently. In *The Republic* Plato claimed that a
fair and just society would provide training for everyone to acquire skills
useful to their society and would then require everyone to exercise them.

From the point of view of justice and fairness professionals should:

- provide equal opportunities for colleagues and clients to develop
  and exercise their capacities unless relevant differences between
  people justify doing otherwise

- refrain from putting some people under more pressure than
  others to take on burdens, such as responsibilities, unless there
  are relevant differences between them.

What might such 'relevant differences' be?

So long as people's latent or actual abilities and interests are in carrying
out activities that are desirable or beneficial, then differences in their capacities will not justify giving them unequal opportunities. If people lose their
interest and abilities, professionals should help them regain them as far as is
in their power, but if people lose their capacities for ever, this, of course,
justifies not offering them equal opportunities with others.

So far as burdens are concerned, there are two relevant differences
between people that could justify putting some under more pressure than
others to take on burdens. If individuals have developed their capacities
knowing that doing so would lead to the expectation that they would take
on particular responsibilities, or if they have been given opportunities on the
understanding that they would take on certain tasks, these differences could

justify putting them under more pressure than others. In such circumstances those under pressure have, in a sense, voluntarily put themselves in a position requiring them to take on burdens, so it is not an unfair disregard of their autonomy to do so.

The injustice of allocating benefits and burdens that are not relevant to capacities

We have seen that it is important for justice and fairness that the benefits and relief from burdens that people are given should be relevant to their needs. It is equally important that they should be relevant to their capacities. We can see this in the following scenario, where people are given a benefit (priority for healthcare) because of their capacities (greater intelligence than others), even though the benefit is unrelated to their capacities. As a result, the people who are not given the benefit are dealt with unjustly. They are given the burden of low priority for healthcare, even though this burden is unrelated to their mental capacity.

> When patients are prioritised for renal dialysis, people with normal mental capacities are given priority over those with mental handicaps. This policy may be defensible from a consequential point of view, since society is likely to benefit more from the functioning of people with normal mental abilities than from the functioning of people who are mentally handicapped. But it is an unjust policy. Differences in people's mental capacities are irrelevant to their need for this treatment, and so to make this the criterion for priority is as unjust as it would be to make any other irrelevant factor, such as race, the criterion. The mentally able are being as unjustly advantaged as people given high priority because they are members of a particular race would be.

Giving people benefits that are unrelated to their capacities, their needs or what they deserve implies that their well-being is more important than that of others. Equally, giving people burdens unrelated to their capacities, or to what they deserve, implies that their well-being is less important than that of others. Requiring the mentally weak to carry the unrelated burden of low priority for healthcare implies that their well-being is less important than that of the mentally able.

As already pointed out, professionals sometimes give people benefits unrelated to their capacities because doing so is justified on consequential grounds (in the renal dialysis case greater benefits to society may be expected from doing so). But if professionals decide to give priority on such grounds they should acknowledge that by doing so they treat people unfairly. They should also make clear that their action is only justified because they consider the benefits of acting as they do outweigh the wrongness of this unfairness. By articulating these ethical points they may be able to make a stronger ethical case for more resources (e.g. more renal dialysis machines) since more resources would not only benefit more people but also diminish the injustice of current practices.

An additional problem with giving people irrelevant benefits, or irrelevant relief from burdens, is that it makes some individuals disproportionately advantaged and powerful, since the advantages they have in one area of life (e.g. greater intelligence or greater earning capacity) are used as reasons for giving them advantages in other areas (e.g. better access to healthcare and the services of other professions).

The importance of transparency in professional practice

In this and the previous chapter we have considered some of the main implications of justice and fairness for the professions. How professions should take account of these implications depends upon the nature of their work. One general way of doing so that applies to all professions is to make their procedures as transparent as possible.

Whenever there is a question of treating some individuals – clients or colleagues – differently from others, people are likely to consider a profession's procedures and practices to be fair and just if:

- the differences that are considered relevant to treating individuals differently are made public
- the criteria governing the allocation of benefits and burdens are made public
- the criteria can be seen to have been applied consistently.

For example:

- when promotions are on offer people are likely to accept the system as fair if the criteria for promotion are:
  - public
  - clearly relevant to the work to be undertaken
  - seen to have been applied consistently

- when burdens such as responsibilities and unpopular working conditions have to be distributed, professionals should:
  - make clear why the 'burdens' are necessary
  - make clear the criteria for their allocation
  - enable people to see that the criteria have been applied consistently
  - strive to ensure that, as far as possible, everyone is under similar pressure to perform whatever functions have to be carried out.

The need for professionals to be transparent as possible about their values and obligations is discussed in Chapter 8, p.141.

Chapters 5 and 6 have outlined some of the main issues in deciding how to treat individuals fairly and justly. The next two chapters focus on the demands of the remaining principles integral to fulfilling the role of professionals: to respect autonomy and act with integrity.

Questions

Individuals' deservingness and entitlement

1. Do situations arise in your profession where members assess the deservingness of colleagues or clients for benefits? (Benefits might include promotion, better working hours, training opportunities, access to professional services, and financial support.)

2. Do you think that deservingness should *not* be considered in relation to any of these benefits? If so, which?

3. For those benefits for which you think deservingness should be considered, what criteria of deservingness would you regard as appropriate? What difficulties might there be in ensuring they are applied fairly and justly?

4. How do you think the officers in the following situation should be prioritised for the new post?

   Two police officers apply for a new post that would give the same amount of promotion to each. One has worked conscientiously and, by voluntarily acting as critical friend to junior officers, has enabled others to become good officers. The other has cut corners whenever possible and not been helpful to junior officers. However, the new post involves liaison with the media, and the second officer is better at giving a good impression and at handling enquiries and information.

(a) Is their 'deservingness' relevant to the situation?

(b) Do you think any importance should be given to consequential considerations in this situation?

5. Are there clear criteria by which members of your profession can know who – whether clients or colleagues – is entitled to what? If not, what factors contribute to this lack of clarity? What would be necessary to resolve them?

Individuals' needs:

6. In the following situations consider how (a) the individuals or groups concerned, (b) you as a professional with relevant resources, might see the importance of meeting their needs.

> In a culturally complex society it is normal in some cultures for each family of parents and children to have self-contained living quarters. In other cultures it is normal for people to share facilities with members of their extended family or community. The sense of well-being of the first group would suffer immensely if families had to share kitchens with others. Does that give them an essential need to live in self-contained accommodation?

> A young woman grows up with the expectation that she will have children. She then discovers that she cannot have them without medical intervention. Should fertility treatment be regarded as an essential need for her, or merely something she desires? Does your view change if she is a lesbian?

> A young man lives in a culture where masculinity is associated with a muscular physique. He is depressed and has low self-esteem because he is skinny, but does not have the confidence or cash to go to a gym. Is help to do so an essential need of his?

> Some parents of children with Down syndrome say their children need facial cosmetic surgery to avoid social discrimination and to

live as normally as possible. Is this a need that healthcare services should meet?

7. Consider the following situations:

A couple has chosen to have six children. As a result the husband requires more money than his colleagues with fewer children. Is the larger income a need that should be met either by his employers or welfare benefits?

People choose to enter particular careers. Is the education necessary for their career a need that should be met, whatever the career? If their careers are teaching, nursing or the police, should their educational needs be met? If their careers are ballet, philosophy or interior design, should their needs be met?

A senior police officer has overtime to offer colleagues. She knows most of the officers want to earn extra money, and also that some will want the work to give them experience of duties they have not carried out before. However, there is work for only a few. As all the officers are equally qualified, she decides to offer it to those who need it most. However, she becomes bewildered by the different needs they have and cannot decide which are more important. How would you advise her?

(a) Can you distinguish between officers' needs and wants?

(b) Which needs do you think are more essential than others?

The officers need or want the work for the following reasons:

- Some younger officers with several children are struggling financially.

- A single officer is anxious to raise money quickly to compete in an international athletics meeting; his sporting successes have brought favourable publicity to the force.

- Two young graduate officers are despondent at the lack of opportunities for different work experience the overtime would give them as they see this as a hindrance to what they were given to expect would be a quick rise through the ranks.

- A middle-aged officer is saving to take his wife on 'the holiday of a lifetime' to help her cope with a long illness.

- Two officers have become depressed and withdrawn from their colleagues since they were involved in a traumatic incident some months ago; the officer allocating the duties thinks the overtime duties would help them get used to working in a team again, and she knows they would be tempted by the extra money.

(c) Since this situation takes place in a working environment, do you think it would be fair to give priority to career-related needs and wants?

(d) Do you think it would be unfair to take into account some of the factors mentioned?

(e) Having thought about this situation, do you think it would in fact be fairer to base the decision on something other than the senior officer's perception of her colleagues' needs?

General issues:

8. If you had problems in your work related to issues raised in this chapter, are there formal or informal opportunities in your profession to seek advice or to discuss the issues with colleagues?

9. Are there aspects of treating people justly and fairly that are relevant to your profession but which Chapters 5 and 6 do not consider?

10. Are there any legal or professional requirements on members of your profession that are relevant to the issues in this chapter?

Note

1   In this statement we are discussing only differences in what individuals deserve because of differences in their contributions, effort or levels of responsibility. We are *not* discussing differences in what people may need – for example, because of their differing clinical conditions.

Chapter 7

Respecting Autonomy

Respecting people's autonomy means, at its simplest, respecting their views on what they want to do, how they want to be treated and how they want to conduct their lives. In Chapter 3 we saw the obligation of professionals as being to respect people's autonomy as far as is possible within a society in which the legitimate interests of all must be considered. Normally the people in question are their clients, colleagues and others with whom they have professional relationships.[1]

In this chapter we are, of course, looking at *ethical* ideas and obligations, not at *legal* ones. Professionals should ensure they know about any legal or professional requirements upon them in relation to the issues discussed here.

What is meant by autonomy?

People are generally thought to have autonomy if:

- they understand their situation, including the options open to them and the likely consequences of each

- they are free of coercion – that is, they are not being forced or pressured to decide or act in a particular way

- they are not being deceived; deception is a form of coercion since people who intentionally deceive others do so in order to manipulate them.

What is meant by respecting autonomy?

To respect autonomy professionals should:

- not prevent people from carrying out decisions they make for themselves about:
  - what they ought to do
  - what they will do
  - what should be done to them
  - what should be done with information about them[2]
- enable others to make autonomous decisions.[3]

Some people use the term 'autonomy' to include concern for people's interests as well as respect for the wishes and decisions of individuals. According to this view, to respect people's autonomy we must also not adversely affect their interests. This book does not use 'autonomy' to include concern for people's interests. This is because people's wishes sometimes conflict with their interests, and when this happens professionals have to balance their obligation to respect someone's wishes against their obligation to pursue their best interests, so it is not helpful to think of wishes and interests under a single heading. Instead, the obligation of professionals to people's interests is seen as part of the obligation to act with integrity and is discussed in the next chapter.

Respecting autonomy in professional practice

Respecting autonomy – whether of clients, colleagues or others – does not mean letting everyone do whatever they want. Before letting people act as they wish we must first consider whether they actually have autonomy:

- Do they understand their situation?
- Are they free of coercion?
- Are they being deceived?

These questions are important in many professional situations. If, for instance, the very young or mentally confused have little understanding of their situation, they cannot be said to have autonomy that ought to be respected in that situation. In such circumstances it would be irresponsible of professionals to allow them to do whatever they want.

In the following discussion we consider these issues mainly in relation to professionals respecting the autonomy of their clients, but most of the points apply to professionals respecting the autonomy of their colleagues and of others with whom they have professional relationships.

Do people understand their situation?

To understand their situation and make informed decisions individuals must be able to:

- grasp facts (these may be about matters, such as legal, financial or medical, which they are not used to thinking about)

- make causal connections between alternative options and their likely consequences

- comprehend the probability of their long-term consequences

- imagine likely future situations and feelings

- relate all the above to making a decision.

The abilities of individuals to carry out these activities obviously vary with their upbringing and education, their stage in life, their mental state and the familiarity of their situation. Babies and people in comas seem to have no ability to make informed decisions. Young children and people with mental impairments may have them to only a limited extent, and mature people who make decisions that would normally be regarded as well informed may not always be able to think fully about complex and unfamiliar situations. If they are in shock, stressed, experiencing strong emotions or just very tired, people often find it difficult to think clearly about complex matters.

Professionals should not, therefore, regard some individuals as always capable of making autonomous decisions and others as never capable. Rather they should try to ascertain the level of understanding and decision making of which a particular individual is capable in a particular situation. They may, for example, judge an elderly, mentally impaired person quite capable of deciding how he should spend the next hour, but not whether he should have residential care or live at home.

Deciding the level of understanding someone must have to make an autonomous decision in a particular situation can be difficult. It is often unreasonable to demand that a person must be able to show a full grasp of all the issues, however complex, before he or she is regarded as capable of making an autonomous decision. It is normally reasonable to accept someone's decision as autonomous if he or she:

- is aware of the aspects of their circumstances that are most important in the professional situation

- understands the main implications and consequences of the options open to them.

Consider the following:

> An elderly widower who lives alone has had a slight stroke and heart attack and is now in hospital. He tires very quickly, needs help in dressing, and finds it difficult to go up and down stairs. Before he is discharged a social worker suggests he should consider leaving his family house and moving to a flat where there is a warden to help residents. The widower becomes very angry, and refuses to consider it, saying he can manage in his family home with someone coming in to help him. His social worker is doubtful whether this is so, and whether he can realistically assess the difficulties he will encounter and his abilities to deal with them. She sees him as too dominated by his desire to return to the normality of his home and wonders whether she ought to try to persuade him to change his mind. She knows he feels dependent on her goodwill, so she is in a strong position to influence him. Should she accept his decision or not? Is there anything else she should do?

She could ask the man how he would cope if certain things occurred. This would encourage him to think realistically about his circumstances, and help her to judge both his ability to deal with any problems and the extent to which his wish to stay in his house is an informed one. She would then be in a better position to decide how much importance to give to her obligation to protect him from harm as against her obligation to respect his autonomy.

Sometimes people regard others as deluded and incapable of making autonomous decisions because they have beliefs that are not part of any familiar religious or cultural perspective. For example, if the elderly man believed he could communicate with his dead wife when he was in the family home, some people might regard him as deluded. But such beliefs would not in themselves make him incapable of making autonomous decisions. Whether he can do so in relation to his situation depends far more upon whether he understands and knows how to cope with practical problems than upon such beliefs. Moreover, just because someone's beliefs are unusual they should not be regarded as necessarily less sensible and less reasonable than beliefs that are more familiar and respected.

A young woman rejects the offer of psychotherapy because she believes her problems will be solved through talking to her recently deceased aunt. Someone else rejects similar help because she says she will pray to the Virgin Mary. Are we entitled to regard the first person as deluded and incapable of making autonomous decisions about her situation but not the second?

Enabling people to understand their situation

As we saw at the beginning of this chapter, many people think that part of respecting someone's autonomy involves enabling them to make autonomous decisions. This view is particularly strong in many professions, such as social care, which seek to empower clients to make their own decisions.

Generally speaking, if professionals consider people do not have a good understanding of their situation, they should do what they can to help them. Indeed, in many circumstances professionals are the only people who can do this, and clients may have sought their services specifically for that purpose.

The responsibility to promote people's autonomy gives professionals an obligation not only to be as well informed as possible themselves, but to inform clients as fully and objectively as possible. This can sometimes be difficult. It is, for example, not easy to convey complex information about issues the recipients are not used to thinking about – especially if they are stressed, ill, very young or old, or of limited intelligence.

It may be thought ideal for professionals to give all the information they have, since they then avoid the danger of selecting information in a biased way and so influencing their clients. However, there are several reasons against professionals always giving everyone all the information they have.

First, giving people all the information may overwhelm them. They may end up less aware of the salient points – and so less able to make an informed decision – than if they had been given less information. Second, it can be difficult to reduce to a manageable amount the knowledge professionals have gleaned from years of experience and expertise. One way of tackling these problems is to give people written information they can reflect upon at their own speed, discuss with others and then ask further questions. Written material can also help overcome the danger of professionals giving biased information.

Third, in some cases it might be thought unnecessarily harmful for someone to have all the information available. For example:

A childless couple in their late thirties seek fertility treatment. Investigations show that there is a very good chance of success, but there also emerges genetic evidence that the husband may become demented in 15 years or so. Should the couple be told of this possibility before they undergo fertility treatment?

In this situation the medical team may feel torn between, on the one hand, enhancing the couple's autonomy by making them as well informed as possible and, on the other, keeping from them the probability of the father's illness, since awareness of it might spoil their enjoyment of their early years with a child.

Once professionals have given as full and objective information as is appropriate, there is then the issue of whether they should give recommendations. To do so without being asked is not compatible with respecting someone's autonomy, for they then run the obvious risk of putting pressure on clients to decide in a particular way. However, if a client asks professionals what they recommend, they respect the client's wishes by giving their views. In such situations they should make clear the reasons for their recommendations and suggest the client thinks carefully whether he accepts these reasons and whether he shares the values and priorities upon which the recommendation is based.

A student asks a lecturer for advice on the choices he should make for the final year of his degree programme. The lecturer recommends him to take a taught course rather than carry out a piece of independent research, saying she thinks that, given the student's past performance, he will find it difficult to motivate himself and to do the planning necessary for an independent project. The student can then consider whether his desire to do the project will be a sufficient motivation for him to organise and carry out a viable programme of research.

There is often a fine line between giving reasons for a recommendation and influencing or coercing clients into making a particular choice. This is particularly so if clients are dependent upon professionals for their services and fear losing their support if they do not accept the recommendations.

Some people, however, do not want to go through the process of being informed and then being asked to make decisions. They want professionals simply to go ahead and do what they think is best. They may not feel capable of deciding for themselves, or they may have sought professionals' help specifically to avoid having to do so. If it is clear that individuals who take this approach are not being coerced into it by others, professionals should take on the responsibility of making decisions. When a client chooses not to make a decision, that is itself a decision to be respected. Professionals should try to make judgements compatible with any decision the clients themselves might have taken, by getting information about what the clients value and what choices they have previously made. If clients are incapable of talking about these things, professionals may be able to discuss them with their family and friends.

As well as the ethical demand that they respect clients' views as much as possible, professionals must also bear in mind whether doing so would be in a client's best interests, as is discussed in the next chapter.

Are individuals free of coercion?

As well as ensuring they do not themselves influence or coerce clients, professionals should consider whether their clients are being influenced or coerced by others. But what level of freedom and independence from external influence should professionals look for?

They cannot expect an individual's wishes to be totally independent of all identifiable influences whatsoever, since we are all inevitably affected by the values of whatever community we come from. Even if we rebel against these values, our rebellion is based on values we have derived from our experiences in that and other communities; no one can be free of all influences. Most of us can identify the influences on many of the decisions we make, but we may still regard those decisions as autonomous. For example, when we are aware that our decisions are the same as those our friends would make in our situation, we nonetheless regard them as our decisions and want others to do the same. So when professionals think a client's wishes show the influence of his or her family, community or culture they should not automatically think the client lacks autonomy or is subject to coercion.

Perhaps the best professionals can do is to look for evidence of people being subject to specific pressures or deception – whether by individuals or groups – that are directly relevant to the wishes they express. They should also look for evidence that individuals want something different from whatever their religious, cultural, family or social values and expectations demand of them. If they do not find such evidence, they should accept their wishes as autonomous. For example:

> A man expresses the wish not to be given a blood transfusion which is essential for his life to continue. He understands the need for the blood

and the consequences of not having it. He and his family are members of a church that considers it is wrong to take into one's body the blood of others. Should the healthcare team simply accept his decision as autonomous or try to explore his ideas more?

If possible the team might talk to him with a view to finding out whether:

- he genuinely believes in the wrongness of taking blood

- he wants to go on living and would accept the blood if there were no community or family pressures upon him.

If there is evidence that if he were on his own he would accept the blood, the team might suggest he thinks again about his decision not to take it.

In such situations professionals have the tricky task of trying to assess how the views of individuals relate to the circumstances and influences surrounding them.

If professionals are satisfied someone's decisions are autonomous, should they respect them?

If professionals are satisfied that someone has a good understanding of her situation and is not subject to coercion, the question then arises as to whether they should go along with whatever decisions she makes. Before thinking about this question in relation to professionals, we look at it generally. Consider the following scenario:

My friend has had ten years of misery living next to a family who make a lot of noise day and night. The teenagers play loud music, and the father, a do-it-yourself fanatic, hammers and uses electric drills until the early hours. All appeals to them to be more considerate and all attempts to curb them by law have proved fruitless. My friend confides that, after much thought, he has decided to move house, but that, after he has done so, he will burn down the neighbours' house – the two houses are not attached – when there is no one at home. He thinks he can make it look like an electrical fire, so arson will not be suspected. He knows all the risks and likely effects on himself and the neighbours and calmly says it is the just and appropriate response: he will destroy what they most value, since they have for ten years destroyed what he most values, the enjoyment of his own home. This act of revenge will help him be reconciled to having to leave the house he loves. He shows no sign of mental disturbance or delusion; indeed he makes clear and balanced judgements in all situations.

My friend has surely made an autonomous decision. No one is coercing him and his decision can be seen as a logical, if unconventional, way of coping with his situation. So am I bound to respect it? I may not like it, but am I entitled to interfere with his decision, say by trying to persuade him to act differently or by warning him that I will report what he intends to do to the police?

A widely accepted view is that a person's obligation to respect the autonomy of others should be tempered by concern for consequences, in particular by considering whether their actions would harm themselves or others. However, John Stuart Mill, in *On Liberty*, took the view that:

> the sole end for which mankind are warranted, individually or collectively, in interfering with the liberty of action of any of their number, is self-protection. The only purpose for which power can be rightfully exercised over any member of a civilised community, against his will, is to prevent harm to others. His own good, either physical or moral, is not a sufficient warrant. (Mill 1974, p.68)

We now consider this issue in relation to professionals.

Mill's view – that we are not justified in interfering with people's actions in order to protect their interests – does not normally apply to professionals since their obligation to integrity requires them to work for the best interests of their clients. So, if clients make decisions which professionals think go against the client's interests, they should normally point this out to them, giving their reasons.

But what, from an ethical point of view, should professionals do if what clients still want to do is likely to harm themselves or others? And what should they do if they fear colleagues' wishes may have harmful consequences?

Given the complexity and variety of situations possible, it is impossible to give specific answers to these questions. However, some considerations arising from the following examples are worth reflecting on.

Weighing clients' wishes against their own interests:

> A young married man has cancer. There are two forms of treatment available: surgery and radiotherapy. Their long-term success rates are likely to be the same, but surgery will make him sterile and impotent.

His present reaction to the illness is that he wants to go for surgery, as he hopes this will get rid of the disease quickly, but his doctor fears he underestimates the likely long-term emotional effects on his marriage. What should the doctor do?

Weighing clients' wishes against the interests of others:

A young man is being treated for stress by a psychotherapist. His problems began when he was being sexually harassed at work by a senior female member of staff. Because he has moved offices, the harassment has ceased, but he is still so angry about the effects it has had on him that he resolves to write to the woman's husband and tell him what went on. He realises this will do considerable damage to her marriage and family, but he thinks it will help him to put others through stress as great as his own. His psychotherapist does not know whether it would help him. Moreover, she cannot decide whether her obligation to prevent harm to others in this situation should outweigh her obliga-tion to respect his wishes – and his possible interests. Should she try to dissuade him from going ahead?

Weighing colleagues' wishes against their own interests and the interests of clients:

An ambitious young police officer wants to go on a training course about working with the bereaved. While he rightly judges having done the course would make him a stronger candidate for promotion, the officer in charge of training knows he has, in the past, been insensitive to the plight of others. The applicant acknowledges this, but argues that the training would help him overcome the problem. The training officer thinks there may be some truth in this, but she knows that once officers have received bereavement training they must be ready to deal with some very difficult situations. She fears the applicant may not handle them well. She tells him he might cause unnecessary suffering to members of the public as well as damage his career prospects, but the young officer still wants to take the course. Should the training officer agree to his doing so?

In such situations professionals should generally be wary of thinking they have greater knowledge of the interests of clients, colleagues and others than their expertise, experience and knowledge of individuals' circumstances warrant. While doctors may well have better knowledge than their patients as to what is in the interests of their physical health, they may not have greater insight as to what is in the interests of their emotional well-being. So in the first case the doctor might not try to dissuade his patient from going for surgery, but simply tell him about the experience of other patients after both surgery and radiotherapy. He might also advise him to think carefully about the long-term effects on his marriage of both options.

In situations like the second, however, when professionals are certain that harm to others will be considerable, instead of merely advising clients to think carefully about their options, they should seriously consider dissuading or, if possible, preventing them from acting as they wish. However, when they are not certain that the harm to others would be substantial, professionals should be wary of seeing their obligation to prevent harm to others as greater than their obligations to their clients' autonomy and interests. (Professionals' responsibility to their clients' interests is discussed in Chapter 8.)

In the third situation the training officer is concerned with the importance to give to a colleague's autonomy and interests. Since the primary objectives of professions are concerned with the well-being of clients rather than of professionals themselves, the obligation of professionals to the autonomy of their colleagues may normally be seen as less strong than their obligation to the autonomy of clients. This being so, in this case as the training officer is not certain that respecting her colleague's wishes would in fact be in his interests, she may well see her obligation to prevent harm to others as outweighing her obligations to him. You are invited to consider these situations further on p.123.

This third situation raises the matter of the autonomy of professionals and in the rest of this chapter we consider issues related to this.

The autonomy of professionals

There are two aspects to the autonomy of professionals – their personal and their professional autonomy. Their personal autonomy consists in their decisions based on their personal views and values, and their professional autonomy consists in their decisions based on professional values and on other factors integral to their professional situation.

Personal and professional values in professional contexts

As we saw in Chapters 2 and 3, professions cannot operate successfully unless their members share the ethical values integral to their role. Inevitably, therefore, when people are working as members of a profession their personal autonomy is circumscribed to the extent that they must comply with professional values and put aside any conflicting personal values. Although this is a restriction on them, it is an ethically acceptable restriction so long as they understand that when they join a profession they are expected to uphold certain values. This gives professions an obligation to ensure their values are clear to those who consider joining them so they can make informed, autonomous decisions about doing so. As we shall see in the next chapter, professions should also make their values known in order to fulfil their obligation to act with integrity.

For most people there may not be any conflict between the fundamental values of their background and those integral to the professional role, since the professional values occur in most major religious and secular traditions. Most religions, for example, consider we should be mindful of the likely results of our actions and should aim for particular objectives – such as enlightenment, eternal life, a good relationship with our god or a just and loving religious community. Many religions also have parables and stories about the importance of striving to bring benefit and avoid harm to our fellow creatures. In secular traditions, too, since at least the fifth century BC, people have claimed we have an ethical obligation to consider the effects of our actions and to prevent harm. Plato, in the story of the man who borrowed an axe (p.49), is concerned with whether the borrower has a greater moral obligation to keep his promise or to prevent harm by keeping the axe. Moreover, some secular thinkers consider that the concern for results is our main ethical obligation – a point of view discussed in Chapter 10, Note 1.

The importance of acting with integrity and fairness is found in many religions. In Judaism, for example, acts such as keeping covenants, being honest and treating people fairly by applying the law impartially are seen as valuable. The goodness of keeping promises and being honest is emphasised in Islam, while telling lies is regarded as wrong in Buddhism, Sikhism and Christianity. Judaism, Islam and Sikhism commend societies in which the 'fruits of the earth' are distributed fairly. Fairness and acting with integrity are also valued in many secular theories of ethics.

Respect for autonomy, however, is not as common in religious and secular traditions as are concerns for fairness, integrity and results. Within many religions there are sects that consider people should give unquestioning obedience to divine authority and not make autonomous decisions. Many members of these sects regard it as wrong to tolerate lack of obedience in others, and some consider they are entitled to impose their ideas on people whose views differ from their own. Similarly, within secular thought, some people (for example, some Marxists) consider that individuals should not question the demands of a regime if it pursues particular social objectives.

These considerations indicate that, while almost all people entering professions are likely to come from backgrounds that have values reconcilable with seeking the best results, treating people fairly and acting with integrity, some people may have values at odds with respecting autonomy. Fundamentalist Christians or Muslims, for example, who consider that everyone should conform to certain religious precepts, may find it difficult to respect the autonomy of people whose behaviour does not comply with these precepts. If these fundamentalists were to become healthcare professionals they might find it difficult, for instance, to refrain from condemning or trying to influence the sexual practices of promiscuous patients.

The possibility of such situations again draws attention to the need for professions to make clear to those who consider joining them the values of the profession and how they are generally applied. Equally, people who think their personal views and values may be irreconcilable with professional ones should consider carefully whether they should join a profession.

When acting in a professional capacity people must be prepared to put aside personally held values and cultural attitudes if they are incompatible with the values of their profession or its objectives.

The extent to which professionals' personal values may be accommodated by professions

It is sometimes possible for professions to accommodate members' personal views and values that diverge from the way professional values are normally applied, provided that doing so does not prevent the objectives of the profession from being achieved and does not adversely affect the delivery of its services.

Here are two examples of when it is possible to accommodate professionals' personal views:

> Some nurses regard terminating a pregnancy as killing a person, and so object to the importance the law and their profession give to respecting the wishes of pregnant women. The nursing profession is often able to accommodate their views by allowing them to opt out of proce-

dures connected with terminating pregnancies. They can do this because:

- these procedures are only part of one area of nursing and so these nurses can contribute fully to the work of their profession without taking part in them

- since other nurses do not object to carrying out these procedures the patients still receive the care they need and the profession's objectives are achieved.

A female Muslim police officer asks to wear a *hijab*, which covers her hair. Although it is not part of the normal uniform she is allowed to so do as it in no way interferes with the performance of her duties.

Here are two examples of when it is not possible to accommodate professionals' personal views:

Some police officers experience dissonance between their personal views and the professional requirement that they treat homosexuals with the same degree of respect they should give to heterosexuals. Some officers find this difficult for a variety of reasons: because they regard homosexuality as a perversion of human nature, or because their religion regards homosexual acts as sinful, or simply because they dislike homosexuals. Given the unpredictable nature of police work, it is not possible to ensure these officers never have to deal with homosexuals. This being so, the police service is entitled to require these officers to act with respect towards homosexuals and to set aside their personal values and attitudes.

A Muslim nurse wishes to wear a *chador* when on duty in a hospital ward. She is allowed to do so for a trial period to see how it affects her work. It is found that some non-Muslim patients – particularly the old, the confused and children – are frightened by her appearance, and that some feel they cannot relate to her because they cannot see her face. Even though she treats the patients well it is clear that some are not comforted or reassured by her attention. Since one of the objectives of nursing on a ward is to give care and comfort to patients it is decided that wearing the *chador* interferes too much with the objectives of her work and her request is rejected.

Professions are entitled to require members to put aside their personal values and views when it is not possible to accommodate them in ways that are compatible with professional values and objectives, and with the proper delivery of services.

Because professionals must be prepared to put aside personal values when they are incompatible with professional considerations, these values are normally not acceptable reasons for challenging the autonomy of colleagues or clients. To use personal values in this way would give them priority over professional considerations. Reasons for professionals to challenge the autonomy of others are likely to be acceptable only if they are based on professional values or on factors integral to the professional situation.

For example:

> A homosexual man with cardiac problems has erectile dysfunction and wants his doctor to prescribe drugs to overcome the problem.
>
> If the doctor does not want to prescribe the drugs because of her personal beliefs that homosexual activity is immoral, she does not have an acceptable reason for refusing the patient's request. In such a situation she might consider whether it is possible to refer the patient to a colleague who does not have the same beliefs. If referral is not possible she should disregard her personal beliefs and give priority to respecting the patient's autonomy.
>
> If, however, the doctor does not want to prescribe the drug because her interpretation of research is that the drug has potentially damaging side effects for someone with the patient's cardiac condition, her reasons for not complying with his wishes are ones that are integral to his condition and the professional situation. They are not a matter of her personal values or beliefs. In this case she should explain to him her reasons for not wanting to prescribe the drug. If he still wants it, she might see whether it is possible to refer him to a colleague who interprets the research differently. If that is not possible she may justifiably consider refusing the patient's request. Since the grounds for her refusal would be her obligation to safeguard the patient's long-term interest – which she regards in this situation as more important than her obligation to respect his wishes – her judgement would be based on applying professional values to professionally relevant factors. In refusing to prescribe the drug she would, therefore, be exercising her professional autonomy.

Just as professionals' personal values are not normally acceptable reasons for challenging the autonomy of colleagues or clients, so they are not normally acceptable reasons for challenging the practices of colleagues. Professionals are entitled to object – and may even be entitled to blow the whistle – if their colleagues' practices conflict with professional values and accepted practices, but they are not normally justified in objecting if they conflict with their personal values only.[4]

Of course, before challenging colleagues' practices professionals should, if possible, discuss with them their reasons for acting as they do. There may be factors that justify their colleagues deviating from accepted practices and that make their actions appropriate ways of applying professional values. On the other hand, colleagues may not have been aware of all the implications of their actions, and may be grateful for the chance to reappraise their practices once the implications are pointed out.

Professional autonomy in relation to client autonomy

The last example brings to the fore the importance of professional autonomy in relation to client autonomy.

Traditionally many professions have taken a paternalistic – or, more correctly, parentalist – view of the professional relationship, seeing the role of professionals as to use their expertise to make decisions, and the role of clients to comply with them. In recent decades, however, as greater emphasis has been given to consumer rights, and as the questioning of authority has increased generally, there has been a change in the way many people view the professional/client relationship. Some consider that clients, not professionals, should have the final say, and some think the relationship should be a partnership in which, if necessary, decisions are reached through negotiation and compromise.

The partnership model of the professional/client relationship is the most acceptable one from the point of view of respecting autonomy, since it acknowledges the importance of the views of both parties. However, professionals must also bear in mind their other ethical obligations and be aware of any legal requirements, since they may be legally prohibited from acting against their clients' wishes. Healthcare professionals in the United Kingdom, for example, may be charged with assault if they treat patients without having, first, if possible, obtained their consent to do so.

Threats to professional autonomy

Professionals must constantly make autonomous judgements since even when there are professional rules of thumb or guidelines from advisory committees relevant to their situation they may have to decide how to relate them to their particular circumstances. Moreover, when ethical principles make incompatible demands, professionals – in discussion with clients and colleagues if appropriate – may have to decide which demands to give priority or how to find an acceptable compromise between them. This is discussed in Chapter 10.

Sometimes, however, the autonomy of professionals is threatened by pressures from society, governmental policies and the organisations that employ them. For example:

- judges may be under pressure from government policy to pass prison sentences on certain types of offender

- healthcare professionals may be under pressure to ensure no one is kept on a waiting list beyond a certain length of time

- university lecturers may be under pressure to award only a small percentage of fails and lower-class degrees

- accountants may be under pressure to pass a company's accounts because the company is a major client of their employers.

Such pressures challenge professionals' autonomy. Judges may consider that the prison sentences for some offenders that are required by government policies do more harm than good. Doctors may think it medically important to treat some patients who have not been long on the waiting list before some who have. Academics may consider that more than a certain percentage of students in a particular cohort do not merit a good-class degree, and accountants may doubt the probity of the accounts.

If professionals resist these pressures it may well make life difficult for them, their colleagues and their employers. On the other hand, if they accede to them they may damage the interests of their clients and the reputation of their profession, and destroy their integrity as professionals.

Professionals whose autonomy and integrity are threatened in these ways have an obligation to point this out to the powers responsible. Conversely, managers of an organisation or profession whose policies threaten the autonomy of its members have an obligation to review their policies and to consider their implications with the members affected. Ideally, of course, they should have procedures in place so that such considerations take place before policies are implemented.

We look at threats to the integrity of professionals, and at what they might appropriately do in the face of them, in the next chapter.

Questions

1. In your profession is it normal practice to:

    (a) tell the people you work for – clients, students, patients, members of the public, etc. – what is going to happen next

    (b) inform them of alternatives and ask for their views

    (c) to do either (a) or (b) depending on the circumstances?

2. If (a) is normal practice, is that because (b) and (c) are not possible, given the nature of the professional situations, or simply because (a) is the customary way of doing things in your profession?

3. Do you think the normal practices of your profession in relation to respecting the autonomy of clients are ethically defensible? Are there situations you think should be handled differently? If so, what are your reasons?

4. Do you sometimes find it difficult to judge whether someone's expressed wishes are based on sufficient understanding of their situation?

5. Do you sometimes find it difficult to decide how much, and how effectively, to inform people so that they can make well-founded decisions? If so, how can you overcome this difficulty?

6. Are people – clients and colleagues – sometimes under pressure from others (including you) to take a particular course of action, when you suspect they may not wish to do so?

7. Do you sometimes feel torn between complying with someone's wishes and taking a course of action that would be more beneficial to the interests of the people who may be affected by what you do? If so, what sort of considerations would be relevant to deciding what you ought to do?

8. What do you consider the ethically appropriate actions for the professionals to take in the three situations outlined on pp.114–115?

9. Do you think the normal practices of your profession in relation to respecting the personal and cultural attitudes of colleagues are ethically appropriate? Are there situations you think should be handled differently? If so, what are your reasons?

10. Do you think the normal practices of your profession in relation to respecting the professional autonomy of colleagues are ethically appropriate? Are there situations you think should be handled differently? If so, what are your reasons?

11. Does your profession provide guidance on issues to do with respecting autonomy?

12. If you have problems in your work that relate to issues raised in this chapter are there opportunities in your working environment to seek advice or to discuss the issues with colleagues?

13. Are there aspects of respecting people's autonomy relevant to your profession that this chapter does not consider?

14. Are there any legal or professional requirements on members of your profession that are relevant to the issues in this chapter?

Notes

1   The obligation of professionals to respect autonomy does not normally extend to a wider circle than this. However, professionals should support those aspects of their society that enable people in general to be autonomous, such as universal education and suffrage.

2   This chapter does not consider the issue of respecting people's views about what should be done with information about themselves. This is dealt with in Chapter 8 in the section on confidentiality.

3   In addition to these two points, some people consider we truly respect people's autonomy only when we refrain from interfering with their decisions because we think it is valuable for them to exercise their autonomy and *not for any other motive*. Such people consider we do not really respect someone's autonomy if our motivation for not interfering with their wishes is consequential – if, for example, we are motivated by the hope that by acting on their wish they will benefit themselves or others. However, since professionals have an obligation to seek the best results, they cannot be censured if their motive for not interfering with someone's wishes is that they think there are consequential reasons for not doing so.

4   Whistle-blowing is discussed in Chapter 8.

Chapter 8

Acting with Professional Integrity

At the end of Chapter 3 the principle for professionals to act with integrity was described as 'to act in accord with the stated or implied values, undertakings and objectives of the profession'.

Acting with integrity basically means having one's actions integrated with one's values. People act with personal integrity when their actions are integrated with their personal values – that is, when there is no inconsistency between what they do and their personal values. People act with professional integrity when there is no inconsistency between what they do and their professional values.

However, as we noted in Chapter 2 and the last chapter, there can be differences between someone's personal and professional values. Ideally, of course, their values would be compatible, so there would be no tension between them. But if there is tension, to act with integrity professionals must comply with professional values, and if tension between their personal and professional values is too great for their peace of mind, they should consider leaving their profession.

What does 'acting in accordance with the values, undertakings and objectives of a profession' entail? When organisations claim to be a profession, and when individuals claim to be members of a profession, they imply, and sometimes explicitly state, that:

- they have the appropriate expertise, powers and resources to promote the objectives of that profession

- when pursuing these objectives they will comply with professional standards and practices

- they will keep confidentiality and respect privacy

- they will be truthful
- they will work for the interests of those who use their services.

People trust professionals to fulfil these implications, and professionals act with integrity when they strive to do so to the best of their ability. In this chapter we look at the demands of these implications.

The most extensive discussion in this chapter is about confidentiality and privacy, since many professionals seem increasingly uncertain as to their responsibilities in this area. If you do not want to consider these issues at this length, feel free to note the text in shaded boxes and move on to Part Three.

In this chapter we are, as in every chapter, looking at *ethical* ideas and obligations, not at *legal* ones. Professionals should ensure they know about any legal or professional requirements upon them in relation to the issues discussed here.

Having the appropriate expertise, powers and resources, and complying with professional standards

The initial responsibility of individuals for having appropriate expertise and powers is usually a matter of them successfully completing qualifications and training programmes before joining a profession, and the powers they need are normally conferred upon them on joining. After joining, professionals have the responsibility to remain up to date; this can be difficult if they are under pressure from other demands. It may also be difficult for them to ensure they have the appropriate resources, since in many organisations they may not have the power to obtain them. For example:

> College lecturers are usually able to ensure there are up-to-date learning resources in the library but they rarely have the power to secure larger facilities, such as laboratories. For these they rely on decisions by others within their institution.

Problems to do with resources often arise because individuals within an organisation have different professional priorities. For some, such as nurses, lecturers and social workers, their priority is to have all the resources – including all the time – necessary to carry out their functions to the appropriate professional standards, while the priority for their managers is to achieve the most efficient use of the organisation's resources. If managers do not know – or are sceptical about – what their colleagues need to operate properly, they have professional reasons to provide the minimum resources they think necessary. In such circumstances, the obligation to integrity of professionals who are not themselves managers is to make the case for the resources they need, and to do what they can to obtain them. They should make clear that without specific facilities they cannot comply with accepted standards of good practice.

The ability of professionals to comply with standards of good practice may also be impaired by factors which we saw in the last chapter can put their professional autonomy at risk. For example:

> It is in the interests of a university to obtain a certain percentage of good degrees, whereas lecturers have a professional obligation to grade work according to academic criteria, regardless of the effect this may have on the overall results of their institution.

> It is in the interests of a hospital to have as great a throughput of patients as possible, and so doctors may be under pressure to discharge patients as soon as possible, thereby risking the objectivity of their clinical judgements.

Such conflicts can damage the professional integrity of both managers and non-managers. If managers employ people to make professional judgements, but then interfere with their ability to do so, they put at risk their own integrity as well as that of their colleagues. This is because, as managers, they fail to fulfil both the undertaking implicit in employing the professionals – that they are hired to apply their expertise – and the undertaking to those who use the services of their organisation – that they will be dealt with according to professional standards. People with managerial responsibility in professions should be mindful of their obligations to their own professional integrity. These include:

- honouring the implied promises made to colleagues in employing them

- honouring the implied promises of their organisation to clients when professional services are made available to them.

When balancing their obligation to integrity in relation to their obligation to seek the best results, people with managerial responsibility should also be mindful of the need to avoid harm to colleagues caused by the stress of conflicting managerial and professional expectations.

When people's ability to comply with professional standards is impaired in these ways, professionals – both managers and non-managers – have an obligation to deal with the problem. They should obviously try to do this within their organisation, but it may be necessary to refer to professional bodies or other agencies. (See the section below on 'Disclosure and whistle-blowing'.)

Sometimes, of course, professionals fail to comply with standards of good practice because they think that it is right to do so in their particular circumstances. If ever this happens, they should be able to say why they think it right to do so, citing countervailing ethical obligations and any other professionally relevant factors.

Even in the most well-equipped and well-run organisations profession-als may encounter situations in which they do not have the expertise or facil-ities to meet professional standards. When this happens, integrity requires them to be honest. If they cannot provide what is necessary, they should inform those using their services and help them gain access to professionals who can – even if they are in rival organisations!

Respecting confidentiality

There are two main areas of confidentiality in professional life:

1. Confidentiality with respect to information about communities, those for whom professionals deploy their expertise – their patients, students, clients, etc. – and participants in research.

2. Confidentiality with respect to the workings of the profession (i.e. communications, administration and policies).

There are ethical reasons for keeping and for breaching confidentiality in both of these areas. The degree and level of confidentiality it is appropriate to keep can be judged only by considering the relative importance of these reasons in specific situations. In this section we look at some of these reasons.

Confidentiality in relation to information about communities, those for whom professionals deploy their expertise, and participants in research

There are reasons on grounds of integrity, concern for consequences, and autonomy to keep this information as confidential as possible. These reasons are as follows:

- In many professions – medical, nursing, counselling, legal and police – professionals cannot give advice or reach judgements that make full use of their expertise unless they have obtained detailed information. Research projects, too, are valueless unless participants give extensive disclosures. Consequently professionals are dependent on people giving information. Since it may be harmful to communities, clients or participants if the information gets into the wrong hands, to obtain disclosures professionals must undertake to keep information confidential. To act with integrity, they must keep this promise.

- If beneficial objectives are unlikely to be achieved without full disclosure of information by clients or others, and if they are unlikely to give it without assurances of confidentiality, there is a strong consequential reason to make and keep these assurances.

- As pointed out in the previous chapter, part of respecting someone's autonomy is abiding by their informed decisions as to what should be done with information about themselves. If people do not want this information to be divulged to others, professionals have an obligation not to do so.

The reasons for professionals to breach confidentiality are mainly based on consequential grounds: to prevent harm or bring benefit, which cannot be achieved in any other way.

For example, professionals may consider they have ethical reasons for breaking confidentiality about what a client is doing or intending to do if they are likely to prevent harm to the public or provide the police with evidence of ongoing crime by doing so. Most may, in fact, have a legal duty to pass on information in such circumstances. Police officers, for instance, may have a legal duty to report evidence of illegal activities when they have been given the information in confidence, and doctors have a statutory duty to notify certain communicable diseases.

So far as breaching confidentiality to promote benefits is concerned, professionals are most likely to be justified in doing this when sharing information with colleagues will promote their clients' interests (e.g. in case conferences in social work). Indeed, many professional procedures can work effectively only if colleagues share information in this way. In such cases the information transmitted should be no more than is necessary to achieve professional objectives. Moreover, whenever possible it should be anonymised and communicated in a manner that prevents access by people who do not need it.

When information sharing is normally likely to be necessary, to act with integrity professionals should, when appropriate, explain this likelihood to clients, making clear who will have access to the information and why. They should also explain any circumstances that may exceptionally necessitate sharing information more widely than this. Whenever professionals feel there are overwhelming reasons for disclosing information to those who would not normally receive it they should, again when appropriate, inform the person who gave them the information or is the subject of it, explaining the reasons for breaching confidentiality and seeking their agreement if possible.

In research projects potential participants should be given clear undertakings about confidentiality. It should be explained who has, or will have, access to information, whether it is anonymised and how the research findings will be published. If possible, prior to the publication of findings, participants' agreement to their release in the form in which they are to be published should be obtained. If participants are unhappy about the way findings are written up, amendments should be made if possible, and if they think confidentiality or anonymity is breached, that is a strong reason for taking the view that amendments must be made. There may, in fact, be a legal requirement for them to do this.

Confidentiality in relation to communications, administration and policies (CAPs) within a profession or organisation

Communication between professionals includes discussion in committees, informal conversation, e-mail, telephone and letter. Administration is the general arrangements by which an organisation or profession operates – for example, managerial and decision-making structures, terms of reference of committees, criteria and values that inform decision making, protocols, codes of conduct, and so on. Policies are the strategies, plans and objectives adopted by the profession or organisation.

The following are the main ethical considerations for keeping CAPs confidential.

COMMUNICATIONS

There are strong grounds of integrity, consequences and autonomy for keeping communications confidential. Take this example:

> A committee is asked to consider how to improve organisational practices. To do this its members need to have free and frank discussions about actual practices in various sections of the organisation. Open discussion is less likely if members think that what they say may

be disclosed to others inside or outside the organisation. There are, therefore, consequential grounds for professionals to undertake to keep such discussions confidential, and once it is made they have an obligation to keep the undertaking. Moreover, if members wish the information they give to be kept confidential, or at least not to be attributed to them individually, colleagues respect their autonomy by complying with these wishes.

Similar grounds support keeping other forms of communication confidential. If members of a profession communicate by e-mail, letter or conversation, trusting that what they say is confidential, and if their communication is likely to be more effective if they can rely on this, again there are grounds of integrity, consequences and autonomy for keeping their communications confidential.

ADMINISTRATION AND POLICIES

There are grounds of integrity, consequences and autonomy for keeping administration and policies confidential. They are, however, generally weaker than for keeping communications confidential. We will look at these grounds in turn.

- Integrity requires professionals to keep administrative arrangements and policies confidential only if they have explicitly or implicitly undertaken to do so. Such an undertaking is sometimes seen as part of the loyalty people owe to their profession or organisation.[1] However, since professions can normally expect to be held publicly accountable for the general ways they work, members of most professions are unlikely to be expected to make such undertakings. There are, for example, no obvious reasons not to be open about the membership, terms of reference and other general criteria by which examination boards and case conferences operate. There are, however, reasons for not being open about the details of the cases they consider, since these will involve information about clients, and so on. Of course there may be special factors (e.g. intellectual property rights or commercial considerations) that militate against going public about the detailed manner – such as the design of management and knowledge processes – in which administrative and policy procedures are carried out. If disclosing them would result in organisations losing the competitive and professional benefits of improving their procedures, they may have good reason to expect – or to require – their employees to keep these details confidential. Integrity would then require them to do so.

- Consequential considerations could also require such confidentiality. For example, if disclosure of operational details resulted in loss of benefits to an organisation or profession, members might be less inclined to improve their ways of working, and so remain less efficient and less mindful of developing good practices. As a result valuable professional objectives might not be so readily attainable. Such consequential considerations, however, are less likely to be relevant to disclosure of general arrangements.

- Considerations of autonomy can also be relevant to confidentiality about detailed practices. If people have contributed expertise to the development of practices only on the understanding that they will be kept confidential, and if they object to their ideas being made available to others, there is a good case for respecting their wishes.

The following are the main ethical grounds for breaking confidentiality in relation to CAPs.

If CAPs are not compatible with professional values, there may be good reasons for drawing attention to them – either to people within the organisation or profession or outside it. There may, for example, be a case for drawing attention to:

- CAPs that manifest unfair or unjust treatment of people (e.g. by containing racist, sexist or homophobic attitudes, or by unfairly discriminating against individuals or groups)

- CAPs likely to have consequences that are not in the best interests of clients, colleagues, members of the public or society in general

- CAPs that fail to respect autonomy (e.g. by not fully informing people of the situation or not allowing them to make choices when appropriate)

- CAPs that threaten the integrity of the profession, organisation or its members by, for example, not complying with accepted professional standards and other professional understandings.

However, members of professions are generally not justified in breaking confidentiality if CAPs go against any personal values they have that differ from professional ones.

As much as possible, professionals should be honest to clients and colleagues about confidentiality in relation to information and CAPs. They should make clear:

- the level and degree of confidentiality they can offer (e.g. who is normally considered as needing access to information on a professional/confidential basis, and why they need it)

- the reasons why, and the circumstances in which, this normal level of confidentiality may be breached.

DISCLOSURE AND WHISTLE-BLOWING

Before professionals disclose information about CAPs to people who would not normally have it, they should consider the following points.

- Disclosure of CAPs can damage individuals, professional morale and trust between colleagues. Consequently, before disclosure professionals should consider whether their concerns can be addressed by talking to the people who are responsible for the CAPs. Those responsible for them may not be aware of their implications and may be grateful for the opportunity to amend them immediately.

- Before disclosing information about the actions of individuals, professionals should try to ascertain whether their contravention of professional values is deliberate and expected, or unintended and unexpected. If it is unintended or unexpected, then it would be unjust to make disclosures in a way that accuses others of wrongdoing. This is another reason for discussing CAPs with those responsible for them before giving information to others.

- People who disclose information about CAPs should not assume that those responsible for them are blameworthy (see Chapter 11).

- Giving information about CAPs to those who would not normally have it is more likely to be justified if:
  - ○ it is highly likely that harm and unacceptable practices will be averted by passing on the information
  - ○ passing information seems to be the only way of averting problems
  - ○ only the amount of information necessary to achieve the ethically justified objective is passed on, and personal information is withheld if at all possible
  - ○ action is taken to reduce any harm the breach of confidentiality may cause.

- If professionals are certain that they should disclose information, they must then consider whether its recipients should be internal or external to their organisation or profession. Because of the concern to avoid harm, passing information to external people is likely to be justified only after attempts to rectify the problem within an organisation have been exhausted. There is then the matter of to whom it should be passed externally. If there are professional, regulatory or governmental bodies with the authority and expertise to take effective action, they are the obvious recipients. If such bodies do not exist, or are thought inadequate, disseminating information to others on a limited and targeted basis is likely to be ethically preferable – again on grounds of restricting harm – than giving it to the media and general public.

- In general, professionals are unlikely to be justified in informing media and the general public (i.e. whistle-blowing) until they have pursued ways of rectifying the problem by other means. Trust in professions is generally in the public interest, so to risk damaging that trust should generally not be regarded as an early option. On the other hand, damage to trust can also result from professionals not taking sufficient action when they are aware that professional practices lack integrity.

- Whether information is given to someone external or internal, the main ethical consideration for professionals is whether the

> unacceptability of what is going on justifies the possible harm of giving information to people who would not normally have it.

Respecting privacy

Respecting privacy is closely related to respecting confidentiality. Whereas confidentiality gives obligations to those who have information, privacy gives obligations to those who do not have it but are in a position to obtain it.

Professionals respect privacy by not pursuing 'unauthorised access' either to information about people, or to their families, friends or colleagues. Access is unauthorised when permission for access has not been given and when it is irrelevant to the professional process.[2]

Privacy of clients, students, patients, the community, participants in research, and so on

Reasons for respecting and not respecting the privacy of clients are similar to those for respecting and breaching confidentiality.

Ethical reasons for respecting privacy are as follows. To achieve professional objectives members of professions often need access to information related to specific aspects of people's lives. Once they have this access they may be in a good position to ask, speculate about or discover information about areas that are professionally irrelevant. However, it is normally understood that, as professionals, they will not invade privacy in these ways, and people are more likely to give relevant information if they are confident that professionals will not do so. There are, then, grounds of integrity and consequences that support respect for privacy. Considerations of autonomy also support it, since if clients do not wish to divulge information professionals should respect their wishes.

However, there are also ethical considerations – usually consequential ones – that sometimes support the invasion of privacy. Doctors, for example, who would not normally ask patients about their associates, may think they should do so if they suspect the patient or others have certain communicable diseases. And professionals who suspect people are involved in serious crime may think they should find out about activities beyond their normal professional remit. For example, a psychotherapist treating a man for addiction to smoking may inadvertently come upon evidence that suggests he is physically abusing his children. She may think she should find out more before considering whether to pass on her suspicions to the appropriate professionals.

If her suspicions prove correct, she may well have a legal duty to inform child protection authorities.

However, before professionals invade a client's privacy they should consider whether there are other ways of achieving a valuable aim. In some cases, instead of seeking further information they may be able to achieve their objective simply by pointing out the possible implications of information they already have, and leave it to their clients to act accordingly.

> For example, an accountant is aware that a client's financial arrangements give no protection from large tax bills for his dependants. Instead of asking about all the dependants he has, she simply makes plain the effects of the arrangements upon possible dependants and leaves it to him to decide whether to take action.

> When dealing with a patient with HIV, a doctor might point out to him the likely effects on any people with whom he has had sexual relations, and leave it to him to decide what to do.

There are of course limits to the value of this approach. It is obvious that it would not be applicable to the case of suspected child abuse; the accountant may be able to give more accurate and beneficial advice if she knows the full picture of the client's dependants, and the doctor may feel that leaving it to the HIV patient to take action is too risky and that his obligation to prevent harm requires more than this.

If possible, whenever professionals feel it necessary to infringe the privacy of clients they should explain their reasons to the clients and ask their permission to go ahead.

Privacy of CAPs

The reasons for respecting the privacy of professional activities are similar to those for keeping them confidential. Grounds of integrity and autonomy can support privacy, since people often take part in professional activities (e.g. membership of a committee) on the understanding that details of discussions will be private and that others will not seek information about them. Consequential grounds can also support privacy, since in some situations – for example, staff appraisal processes and disciplinary procedures – frank and private exchanges between colleagues may be essential.

However, if there are well-founded suspicions that either the activities of some colleagues or more general professional practices are ethically unacceptable, these suspicions may justify invasion of privacy. Unacceptable practices include:

- unfair or unjust treatment of people
- practices not in the best interests of clients, colleagues, members of the public or society in general
- practices that fail to respect autonomy
- practices that threaten the integrity of the profession or organisation, or its members.

Invading privacy for these reasons is more likely to be justified if:

- whenever appropriate, before privacy is invaded colleagues whose activities are under suspicion are asked for their comments
- those making the investigation are authorised to do so and/or are in a position to take responsible action should they find anything untoward
- action is taken to reduce any harm the invasion of privacy may cause.

Professionals should be honest about the amount of privacy that can be guaranteed to clients and colleagues, making clear:

- the normal level and degree of privacy (i.e. what processes, communications and information are normally considered private)
- the reasons why, and the circumstances in which, this level of privacy may be breached.

Being truthful

Being truthful is a very important aspect of professionals' obligation to act with integrity. People expect and trust professionals to tell them the truth. The main ethical reasons for professionals to be truthful are:

- to act with integrity
- to enable those to whom they communicate – whether clients or colleagues – to make informed autonomous decisions.

The main ethical reasons for professionals not to be truthful are to do with seeking the best results: they may think that better consequences are likely if they do not tell the truth – or, at least, do not tell the whole truth.

There are negative and positive aspects to professionals' obligation to be truthful. These are:

- the obligation not to deceive intentionally
- the obligation to inform appropriately.

The two inevitably overlap, but we will consider them separately.

The obligation not to deceive intentionally

There are different ways in which we may intentionally deceive others. For example:

- lying (i.e. deliberately telling people what we believe to be false)
- deliberately omitting to tell them all that we know that is relevant to their situation
- deliberately not putting them right when they misunderstand their situation.

If deception is ever thought justified because of other ethical considerations (e.g. in order not to cause people unhappiness), lying is usually regarded as the most unacceptable form of deception. This is because making statements one believes to be false to clients and colleagues seems to be the most flagrant abuse of the trust they put in what they are being told.

Here are two situations in which professionals consider that telling lies is worse than being 'economical with the truth':

> Tim, a psychotherapist, is working with a dysfunctional family and sometimes sees the children without their parents. In his conversations with them the children assume they are all the offspring of their mother's husband, whereas Tim knows that some of them are not. Because they never question this assumption they never ask him about their parentage. He has to decide whether he should tell them they are mistaken or whether he should keep quiet, since he fears this knowledge could damage family relationships further.
>
> Tim decides that, so long as the children do not ask him about their parentage, he should say nothing about it. He considers this less bad than if he had to lie to them, which he would see as a flagrant infringement of his obligation to be truthful. Because he sees saying nothing as

less of a breach of this obligation, he considers the wrongness of deceiving the children in this way, by leaving them under a misapprehension, is outweighed by his obligation to prevent harm. However, he thinks that, were the children ever to ask whether they all have the same father, he would probably not be justified in lying to them.

Joan, a doctor working for a charity with a limited budget, tells a patient about two ways of treating his condition. She gives him the advantages and disadvantages of each and asks which he would prefer. She does not say that these are the only two ways of treating him, and at no point does she say anything untrue. However, a third option for treatment is available. She deliberately does not mention this because she thinks the extra resources it would incur, and the added restrictions it would impose on her treatment of other patients, would not be justified by its likely additional benefits to this patient.

Let us look more closely at Joan's situation. Given that she is telling the patient about ways of treating his condition, he might reasonably expect to be told about all of them. By not fulfilling these expectations, Joan is deceiving him and to that extent failing to meet her obligation to act with integrity by being truthful. To have fulfilled his expectations Joan would have had to tell him of the three options and point out that, though the third might be most beneficial to him, in her view it would not lead to the best consequences for her patients overall. Furthermore, to respect his autonomy as well, she would have had to give him this information in a way that did not put him under pressure to accept one of the other two options.

If Joan were asked to account for not telling the patient about all ways of dealing with his condition she might claim:

- that she considered her obligations to truthfulness, to work for best interests of the patient, to respect the autonomy of this patient, were outweighed by the likely benefits to other patients, whose interests she also has an obligation to pursue, of not offering the third option

- that by not mentioning the third option she probably caused the patient less stress than by telling him about its potential benefits and then explaining why she did not want to provide it

- that even though she had infringed her obligation to be truthful she had infringed it less than if she had lied and told him there were only two options.[3]

These situations are not described to recommend the actions taken by Tim or Joan, but to illustrate aspects of the professional obligation not to deceive, and to show the overlap between this and their obligation to inform appropriately. It is this we consider next.

The obligation to inform appropriately

Since people seek the services of professionals to be enlightened as well as to be helped, and since professionals usually undertake to inform, they have an obligation to both enlighten and inform.

There are different ways of informing: professionals could give all the information they have, or only some. However, if all the information they have is too much for people to cope with, the recipients will not be enlightened by being given it all. In the section entitled 'Enabling people to understand their situation' in Chapter 7, we discussed the point that it is sometimes better for professionals to give only selected information in order that people may make autonomous decisions. We also discussed the ethical issues that arise from giving only selected information, so we do not repeat them here.

It is, of course, normal for professionals – lecturers, lawyers, doctors – to select and present information in the way they think appropriate for their audience. For example:

A doctor describing a particular medical condition is likely to select and present information differently when talking to a patient from when she is talking to medical students. When initially telling a patient about his condition she is unlikely to go into all the technical details or to deliver the information in the same way as she would when lecturing. In later discussions with the patient, however, as his familiarity with his condition increases, and as the professional process evolves and decisions have to be made, she may give the patient all the information she has given to students, though she may present it in a different way.

When making judgements about people's abilities to understand, professionals should bear in mind that their abilities may be affected by:

- their general level of intelligence
- the stress they are under
- their familiarity with the issues

- the stage the professional process has reached
- discussions that have already taken place.

So, although what is necessary for professionals to meet their obligation to inform may vary from situation to situation, what is required is not arbitrary, but depends upon their taking account of several factors in each situation. To be truthful in ways that fulfil their obligation to act with integrity, professionals should:

- not intentionally deceive others
- give up-to-date information and be honest about any limitations in their knowledge
- give information that is as full as is appropriate in the situation, bearing in mind recipients' abilities and the objectives of the professional process.

Being truthful about professional values and obligations

One important topic about which professionals should be as truthful and transparent as possible – and one that is frequently overlooked – is their professional values and ethical obligations.

To be truthful and transparent about professional values and obligations is vital to acting with integrity, since it makes clear to people why the undertakings set out at the beginning of this chapter may not always be honoured completely. They will then understand why, for example, total confidentiality may not always be possible, or why professionals may not always be able to work solely for their best interests, as discussed in the following section.

Ideally professionals should make their ethical principles and obligations clear whenever they enter a professional relationship with someone. On some occasions this is, of course, impossible. When a person who is conscious but in urgent need of life-saving surgery is brought into hospital, that is not the moment for the surgeon to explain his ethical stance. There is, however, much that professions and their members can do to make people generally aware of their values, so that when people receive their services, or consider whether to do so, they are better informed. One of the best ways of doing this is for professional bodies to publicise the fundamental values and objectives of their professions, including any ethical codes their members are expected to take account of.

If professional bodies accept the views of this book, they should also explain that their members have general obligations to seek the best consequences, to be fair and just, to respect autonomy and to act with integrity. They should make clear that:

- their members will only *not* adhere to any one of these general obligations if they genuinely consider that, in a particular situation, its demands are ethically outweighed by the demands of the others, or by any legal or profession-specific requirements

- their members will infringe the demands of any of these obligations only if they consider that to do so is the *only* way to meet more important ethical demands or legal requirements

- their members will do what they can to minimise any infringement of these obligations.

Professional bodies should also point out that, as part of their professional accountability, members should be able to give reasons why they consider any ethical obligation they do not fulfil is outweighed by other considerations.

Of course, to act with integrity, professionals must not only publicise these points, but act in conformity with them.

Working for the best interests of the people who use professional services

In many professional areas clients and professionals regard the undertaking to work for the best interests of clients as the most important one professionals make – whether they make it explicitly or implicitly.

Many of the ethical considerations relevant to this undertaking are similar to those for seeking the best results, only in this case the well-being to be pursued is that of the clients rather than of everyone who may be affected by the actions of professionals.

In some professions clients' interests are often seen in narrower terms than well-being. They may, for instance, be seen only in terms of their financial or legal interests. However, even in these circumstances professionals have an obligation to consider how different courses of action might affect clients' well-being overall. Consequently, as we are concerned with the obligations of professionals in general, we see clients' interests in terms of their well-being.

When deciding what they should do to work for the best interests of their clients, professionals should:

- use their expertise to estimate the likely effects of alternative actions on clients' interests

- take into account what clients see as their interests and how they view the acceptability of those effects

- judge which actions are most likely to promote clients' interests in the long term.

If clients are unable to express their views, whenever appropriate professionals should try to ascertain what is, or has been, important to them, by discussing the matter with those who know them well. Taking clients' views into account is also, of course, relevant to respecting their autonomy.

When professionals consider there is a divergence between what they see as in a client's interests and what the client wants, they have an obligation to balance the two and to decide which is more important in the circumstances. There are several things they should consider before reaching their decision as to what to do. If there are legal considerations or relevant guidance from professional and advisory bodies they should consider how they apply to their case. They might also discuss the general issues with colleagues, taking care not to breach confidentiality. Most importantly, they should if possible discuss the issues with the client, explaining why, in their opinion, acting in accordance with his or her wishes would not be in the client's interests and also pointing out that as professionals they have an obligation to pursue the latter. The more the professional relationship operates as a partnership, the more likely it is that the client and professional will find a mutually acceptable way forward. If this is not possible, then the professional has to decide whether, in the circumstances, the obligation to pursue the client's best interests is greater than respecting his or her wishes, bearing in mind, among other considerations, the likely consequences of each. (For further discussion of issues to consider in such situations see Chapter 10, especially p.167.)

As discussed earlier situations may also occur in which professionals see a conflict between what they should do for the best interests of a client and what they should do for the best interests of everyone who might be affected by their actions. In the example on p.139, Joan, a doctor, thinks she can bring about better consequences for her patients overall if she does not do what is in the interests of the patient she is currently treating. In her case, since all the people affected by her actions are her patients, she has an obligation to pursue the best interests of them all. In view of this she decides that the benefits she can bring to her other patients outweigh her obligation to do all she can for the interests of her current patient.

Sometimes professionals are torn between what they see as necessary for the best interests of their clients and what they think will bring the greatest benefits or prevent considerable harm to people who are not their clients. Once again, when legal considerations and professional guidance are relevant, they should consider how they might be applied to their situation, and may seek to discuss the general issues with colleagues. They should also consider whether the apparent incompatibility between the interests of their client and the best consequences for others is as great as they at first perceive, since the people at risk of harm may well be connected to the client, and harm done to them might adversely affect the client. If this is the case, any course of action that risks harming others may not, in fact, be in the client's best interests. In the following example, for simplicity of discussion, we assume there are no relevant legal or professional requirements that prescribe what the professional should do.

> A doctor's patient is an army officer with a degenerative neurological disease. The patient refuses to tell his employers about his condition as he wishes to carry out a particular assignment that would be the high point of his career. The doctor fears that if his patient takes on such a heavy responsibility the stress is likely to exacerbate the disease. This, in turn, could affect his judgement and could put the lives of many people at risk. The doctor has put these points to the patient, but he refuses to inform the army.

The doctor has to decide whether he should inform the army of the patient's condition. From the point of view of seeking the best consequences for others, informing the army would seem to be the right thing to do. At first the doctor thinks it would be against the patient's interest to do this, but then wonders whether it would be. For, although it would result in the patient missing out on the high point of his career, the likely alternative – stress and the possible death of colleagues for whom he is responsible – may be far less conducive to his long-term interests. (We will return to this example in Chapter 9.) On p.168 there is a list of considerations relevant to the issues raised in this section.

If, after bearing in mind such considerations and any relevant guidance, professionals are convinced that pursuing the best interests of their client is incompatible with bringing major benefits or preventing harm to others, before taking action they should reflect on the following ethical considerations.

- In many professions the undertaking to work for clients' interests is probably the most important one they make – whether explicitly or implicitly.

- Unless professionals are confident there is a divergence between their clients' wishes and interests, the wishes of clients are likely to support professionals working for their interests rather than giving weight to any countervailing ethical considerations, such as preventing harm to others.

- Any ethical considerations in favour of not pursuing clients' interests should also be weighed against:
  - harm to the interests of the clients
  - the unfairness of clients not being given what they are entitled to expect, and of being required to sacrifice this for the good of others
  - harm to the professional relationship and to trust in professions by not pursuing clients' interests.

Whenever professionals consider not giving precedence to their obligation to work for the client's best interests, the onus is on them to justify not doing so.

In this chapter we have identified some of the main considerations relevant to acting with professional integrity and seen how they relate to the demands of the other ethical obligations of professionals.

In Part Two we have explored the demands of the four fundamental values that are integral to fulfilling the role of professionals in culturally complex democracies. In Part Three we will consider how these values – expressed as principles – provide an ethical framework for professional practice.

Questions

1. Do you or other members of your profession find it difficult to have up-to-date expertise and facilities? If so, why is this? Would it be ethically appropriate to take any action to overcome the problem?

2. Is it clear which aspects of professional activities you are expected to keep confidential? If so, do you regard these expectations as ethically justified?

3. Are you ever torn between keeping and breaching confidentiality? If so, what considerations support each line of action?

4. Have situations occurred in your profession in which, in your opinion, someone's privacy has been unacceptably invaded? Are you aware of considerations that would support the invasion?

5. Does your profession provide guidance on issues to do with respecting confidentiality and privacy?

6. Could you, your colleagues or your profession do more to make people aware of the ethical considerations that are relevant to your work?

7. If you have problems that relate to the issues raised in this chapter are there opportunities to seek advice or to discuss the issues with colleagues?

8. Are there aspects of acting with integrity that are relevant to your profession but which this chapter does not consider?

9. Are there any legal or professional requirements on members of your profession that are relevant to the issues in this chapter?

Notes

1 When this is the case professionals have, of course, an obligation to keep confidentiality. However, although there are strong reasons (which we have considered) for loyalty to require confidentiality with respect to communications, it is less clear why it should require confidentiality in relation to general practices and policies, since professions can expect to be publicly accountable for the way they work.

2 Some people see respecting privacy as part of respecting autonomy. That is because they consider that respecting a person's autonomy includes protecting

their interests and they see respecting privacy as a way of doing that. However, in the chapter on autonomy (Chapter 7) we specifically excluded protecting someone's interests from being part of respecting their autonomy, because there are times when professionals may judge that a person's interests are not best served by respecting their autonomy. Consequently, we do not see respecting privacy as part of respecting autonomy, although the two are closely related.

3   This situation, where a doctor has to make difficult decisions about the best use of resources on her own, is not put forward as a model of good practice. The more professionals have the support of a team in which they can discuss such issues, or an advisory body that gives general guidelines about such issues, the better.

Applying Values to Practice

In Part One we identified the values integral to the role of professionals working in culturally complex democratic societies and saw that they are best expressed as general principles. In Part Two we explored the obligations these principles give to professionals. In the first two chapters of this part we see how the principles can provide a supportive ethical framework for professionals and be incorporated into their thinking. In the final short chapters we consider how professionals should deal with accusations of blame and claims about rights.

Applying Values to Practice

Chapter 9

A Framework for Ethical Thinking in the Professions

The usefulness of a framework of principles

As we have seen, the principles expressing the values integral to the professional role are:

- to seek the best results

- to treat individuals justly and fairly

- to respect people's autonomy

- to act with integrity.

If arranged differently, these principles provide a useful mnemonic:

- to treat individuals justly and **F**airly

- to respect people's **A**utonomy

- to act with **I**ntegrity

- to seek the best **R**esults

making the word FAIR.

In the hurly-burly of professional life, having a memorable framework of ethical principles is supportive in several ways.

- It enables professionals – working individually or as members of groups such as advisory committees – to identify quickly those aspects of a situation that are ethically important. For example, 'Before we adopt this policy we must consider whether it is likely to achieve the best results and whether it treats the students fairly.' Once professionals have identified the relevant ethical principles they can think how they have been interpreted and applied in previous situations.

- When professionals are uncertain what they ought to do, a framework can help identify the reasons for their uncertainty. It may be that they haven't yet thought out how to apply the relevant principles to their particular circumstances. For example, 'What sort of outcome would constitute the best results in this situation?' Or it may be that they see two or more principles as relevant and are torn between their apparently incompatible demands. For example, 'Should I keep my promised appointment, which will achieve little, or finish this report on time, which will benefit my clients enormously?'

- If colleagues have the same ethical framework they have a shorthand way of referring to the ethical aspects of their situation and have a conceptual structure within which to discuss them.

- Having a framework can remind professionals of ethical considerations that others may expect them to take into account. This can help them to be sensitive to the ethical perspectives of others, and to anticipate the ethical objections and issues that may arise if they follow a particular course.

- Having a framework can remind professionals of the ethical aspects of a situation that they may have overlooked.

- A framework provides a general ethical remit for professionals to focus upon. It helps ensure they do not make evaluative judgements from the point of view of a particular cultural, religious or secular basis.

The following example shows how having this framework of values can be useful.

A British university, which is not affiliated to any religious or secular foundation, provides courses for people from all cultures in British society. It is, therefore, inappropriate for its ethics policy to reflect the values of any particular culture. So the university asks all its personnel to adopt the framework. The principles within it provide the ethical remit of the University Ethics Committee, the deliberations of which involve interpreting and applying the principles to the situations before it.

Members of the committee are not empowered to act in accordance with their personal or cultural values. This is important because, if members promote their personal values, their deliberations will consist in a struggle of personalities and cultures rather than an ethical analysis of situations using agreed values. While members may well have their own personal and cultural values, they do not bring these into the discussion and the committee's decisions are not based upon them.[1]

Appealing to principles

When people are wondering what they ought to do they are concerned with reasons for and against acting in various ways. Ethical principles give them reasons. They are the 'tools of moral reasoning',[2] as the following snatches of conversation illustrate:

'We should allocate more resources to sports facilities for the girls.'
'Why?'
'Because we are being unfair: the boys have much better facilities.'

'What's wrong with my husband, doctor?'
'I'm afraid I can't tell you.'
'Why not?'
'Because I promise my patients that I will keep information about them confidential.'

Here the speakers give reasons for what they ought to do by appealing to principles they think relevant to the situation: that they should treat people fairly and keep promises.

However, by referring to principles people do not just put forward a reason for behaving in a certain way on one particular occasion. They imply that there is a reason for behaving in that way on all occasions that are relevantly similar – that is, that they are 'acting on principle'. By the doctor saying he should keep confidentiality because he has promised to do so, he implies that he thinks *whenever* he has made a promise he has a reason for keeping it. We would therefore expect him to feel obliged to keep a promise on other occasions unless he has countervailing ethical reasons for not doing so. Let us explore the situation of the doctor we looked at at the end of the last chapter to see how this might occur. Again, for the sake of simplicity, we assume that there are no legal or specific professional requirements that prescribe what he should do.

The doctor's patient is a senior male army officer in the early stages of a degenerative neurological condition. The course the disease may take is unpredictable. At present the patient functions well, and few people notice any impairment. He could remain like this for years, but he could also lose competence rapidly and start behaving erratically, particularly if under stress.

When the patient's wife calls the surgery to ask what is wrong with her husband the doctor refuses to tell her, on the grounds that he must keep the promise of confidentiality he has made to her husband. However, he says he will tell his patient that she would like to know what is wrong.

Some months after this conversation the doctor learns that the man is about to take command of an operation that could put at risk the lives of many soldiers and civilians. The doctor realises this will put the patient under stress and discusses with him whether he should go ahead with it. The patient says the assignment will be the high point of his career and he is not going to turn it down. He also refuses to tell the army about his condition. Given the risk of harm to others, the doctor reluctantly decides he ought to do so himself.

Since this decision of the doctor is inconsistent with his earlier decision to keep his promise of confidentiality, it is ethically unacceptable for him to treat the two situations differently unless he has sound reasons for doing so.

The doctor agrees with the principles in our ethical framework, so as well as thinking that he should be mindful of the best interests of his patient and keep his promises, and that he should respect his autonomy, he also thinks that harm should be prevented. In the second situation he considers that preventing harm outweighs the importance of both keeping his promise and respecting his autonomy. He is uncertain, however, whether it would, in fact, be in his patient's interests to take on the assignment as the stress could damage his health still further.

So, when talking to the patient's wife he thought the ethical value of keeping his promise outweighed any harm that might result from not divulging information to her. But in the second situation he considered the likely harm to others was so great that his obligation to prevent it outweighed his other obligations. Because he sees the two situations as different in ethically relevant ways (i.e. danger of loss of life in the second but not in the first situation) he thinks he is right to make different judgements about them, and that he has sound ethical reasons for behaving differently in the two situations.

This example brings out the crucial importance of whether or not situations are seen to be similar in all ethically relevant ways. If they are seen to be similar they will be thought to give rise to reasons for acting in a similar way, but if they are seen to be ethically different they may give rise to reasons for acting differently. This echoes the importance of relevance and consistency in the principle of fairness discussed in Chapter 5 (p.71).

Consequently, if the doctor were to encounter two similar situations again, the only difference being that the patient is now a female officer and it is her husband asking for information, we would expect the doctor to have the same reasons for acting in the same way again – that is, to refuse information to the patient's spouse, but to inform the army. We would expect this if we consider that the swap in sex of patient and spouse does not alter the ethically relevant factors in the situations. Since these factors were that there was no danger to life in the first situation but there was in the second, the changed sex of the spouse does not alter the relevant factors. So if we found that the doctor had informed the husband when he asked about the health of his spouse, but not the wife when she did, and that he did so because they were of different sex, we might think he had discriminated unfairly against her (i.e. he had treated her differently from the man because of differences between them that were irrelevant to the situation). See the discussion of fairness in Chapter 5.

Although people's judgements about what they ought to do imply that they see reasons for acting in a particular way in relevantly similar circumstances, it does not mean that these reasons will in fact hold sway when these circumstances occur later. By that time people may have questioned their previous ethical judgement for ethically relevant reasons – perhaps because the consequences of what they did on a previous occasion were different from those they had anticipated, or because, although the later situation has similar factors to the earlier one, they now realise that other aspects of the situation were ethically more significant than they had first thought, or that there were alternative actions they had failed to consider. For example, the doctor might later think that, once he heard of the patient's assignment, he should have urged his patient to tell his wife about the illness, as she might have persuaded him either not to go ahead with the assignment or to tell the army about his condition.

These considerations show that we expect people to apply their ethical judgements consistently unless they have ethically relevant reasons for not doing so.

Making ethical decisions

By applying principles

As we have seen in the doctor example, one approach to making decisions is to decide which ethical principles are relevant to the situation and then to apply them.

When the doctor was first talking to his patient's wife he considered only one principle relevant – to keep promises – and so he refused to divulge any information to her. The thinking in such simple cases can be expressed as a piece of logic known as a practical syllogism:

First premise (general principle):	Promises ought to be kept.
Second premise (particular fact):	I have promised to keep information about patients confidential.
LOGICALLY ENTAIL	
The conclusion:	I ought not to divulge information about this patient.

Here each premise logically entails the conclusion – that is, if we agree with the premise, we *must* accept the conclusion: we would be illogical if we did not.

This form of reasoning can be seen behind many cases of simple ethical decision making:

First premise (general principle):	A person ought to seek the best consequences.
Second premise (particular fact):	Not giving someone all the information in this situation will cause less suffering, and so produce better consequences, than telling him everything.
LOGICALLY ENTAIL	
The conclusion:	I ought not to tell him everything.

Usually, however, applying ethical principles is not as simple as this. As we have seen in many examples in Part Two, more than one principle may be relevant to a situation and they may conflict. When the doctor's situation developed, he considered that several principles were relevant and there was conflict between them. In addition, as we also saw in Part Two, it may be possible to interpret the principles in different ways. As a result, people may have to decide both how to interpret the principles in their particular circumstances and what to do about any incompatibilities between them. Consequently making judgements in the light of principles is often a much more complex process than the simple deduction of practical syllogisms. It requires what is sometimes called 'practical wisdom'.

Let us look again at two situations we have already considered as examples of practical wisdom.

> Tim, a psychotherapist, is working with a dysfunctional family. In his conversations with the children they assume they are all the offspring of their mother's husband, whereas Tim knows that some are not. He has to decide whether he should tell them that they are mistaken, or whether he should keep quiet, since he fears this knowledge could damage family relationships further. He feels torn between the obligations to be truthful and to prevent harm.

> On the basis of research about QALYs, a health authority committee considers that, to bring the maximum long-term benefit to the population it serves, it should put its resources into education about smoking and healthy eating, and into comprehensive screening programmes. However, it is also aware that people who are currently ill require expensive interventive medicine. The committee's choice seems to be between meeting its obligation to go for the best consequences in the long term and its obligation to the interests of current patients.

In situations like these people often reach a decision in ways that are more subtle and interesting than the practical syllogism. For example:

> Tim decides that, so long as the children do not ask him about their parentage, he should say nothing about it. He considers that this is less bad than if he had to lie to them, which he would see as a flagrant infringement of his professional integrity. Because he sees saying nothing as less of a breach of this obligation, he considers its wrongness is outweighed by his obligation to prevent harm. However, he thinks that, were the children ever to ask him whether they all have

the same father, he would probably not consider he would be justified in lying to them. Tim deals with his dilemma by thinking carefully about what his obligation to act with integrity by being truthful requires in that situation.

The committee decides to concentrate resources on the needs of current patients, but also to explain to the public the nature of the dilemma and why its members have chosen as they have. This publicity is used to encourage schools and the media to run campaigns promoting non-smoking and healthy eating. In this way the committee hopes to go some way to meeting the following obligations:

- To fairness, by treating patients as they are entitled to be treated in relation to their needs.

- To integrity, by attending to its remit as a health authority by working both for the interests of those who are currently ill and for the long-term interests of all its population.

- To results, by alleviating the suffering of current patients and by encouraging others to work for the long-term best consequences of the population as a whole.

You may or may not agree with the conclusions reached by Tim or the health authority committee, but they show people reflecting on how to interpret and apply their principles to their situations. Their lines of thought do not have the compulsion of practical syllogisms, where if people accept a premise they must accept the conclusion. Instead the lines of thought are a series of considerations that make it reasonable to accept the conclusions they lead to.

Making decisions either by following principles, as in a practical syllogism, or by interpreting, applying and prioritising principles as they think fit, are appropriate ways for professionals to make ethical decisions.

In Chapter 10 we take another look at ways of dealing with conflicting principles.

By relating convictions and principles

Appealing to principles does not always work as a way of making decisions. Sometimes people do not know, or cannot decide or agree, which principles are relevant, or how to interpret them, or to which to give priority. Sometimes people get more guidance from a conviction about what it is right to do in a particular situation than from general principles.

How professionals should respond to convictions about particular situations depends upon whether they have time to reflect before taking action. If they have no time to reflect they can only follow their conviction in the hope that it is compatible with their ethical principles. After acting they should take time to reflect on the compatibility between them. They should also consider whether the fact that they had no time to reflect was their fault and, if so, how they could alter their working practices so that this is less likely to happen in the future.

If they do have time to reflect before acting they should relate the conviction about the particular situation to the ethical principles they consider relevant to it. If the conviction is not compatible with the way they normally interpret and apply the principles, they should consider whether they should modify either or both.

Whether they reflect before or after acting, in their reflection they should consider whether:

- the principles should lead them to modify the conviction about the particular situation, or

- the conviction should lead them to modify the way they have previously interpreted or applied the principles.

Here is an example of the first decision:

> A student e-mails a lecturer to ask if she may hand in an essay after the deadline for submission: she had forgotten she had the work to do and so it will not be completed in time. The lecturer's immediate thought is that he should accede to the request as it would show his appreciation of the student's extensive contribution to the success of the course. However, he then thinks that to do so would run counter to his normal interpretation of treating students fairly. This is that he should make exceptions to regulations for students only if there is a factor in their situation over which they have no control and that is relevant to the particular regulation, or if there is a difference between them and the other students that is relevant to the situation. In this case, the student's forgetfulness is not something over which she has no control in the way that illness is, nor is the fact that she makes greater contributions than the other students relevant to submitting her essay late. He refuses the request.

Here is an example of the second decision:

A young lecturer in philosophy uses lectures to take students through lines of thought and their critical appraisal. She sees this way of developing the students' intellectual abilities as the greatest benefit she can give them. One hot afternoon, in front of 30 students, she suddenly feels that what she is doing is not appropriate to the moment. She casts aside her planned lecture and talks generally about the relevance of the theories being analysed to aspects of their lives. At the end of the lecture the class has not completed the task she had set. However, when she later reflects on the afternoon she thinks that what she did was an equally valuable contribution to the students' well-being. She decides she can benefit them not only by enabling them to analyse ideas but by pointing out the relevance of the ideas to modern life.

For professionals to reconsider their ethical views in these ways does not, of course, mean changing them just because they do not feel like carrying them out. It means considering whether there are ethically relevant considerations for questioning their immediate responses or for rethinking how they normally interpret and apply principles.

By being prepared to relate their convictions to a framework of principles, or to question their current interpretations of the principles, members of professions take their ethical obligations seriously.

Can professionals do without principles?

At the end of Chapter 1 we looked at two approaches to ethics that have little, or no, place for principles. We will now look again at these approaches and consider why they would not be appropriate for professionals.

One is the case-study approach, in which people see their ethical thinking as starting from emotional reactions, intuitions or convictions about what it is right to do in particular situations. When they have had several such experiences, they consider whether they are compatible with each other. If they are, they develop tentative general guidelines.[3]

This approach – building up one's ethical views on the basis of emotional experiences, intuitions and convictions – can be an attractive way of developing *personal* ethical perspectives, but it is not suitable for ethics in the professions. Professions have to have values and systems of guidance that are up and running. They cannot fulfil their role properly by operating without acknowledged values or principles until such time as their members have had sufficient convictions about particular situations to build up tentative guidelines.

The other is the moment-to-moment approach. This approach does not attempt to develop guidelines, but simply relies on going along with emotions, feelings, intuitions or convictions of the moment. However, because of the sometimes contradictory nature of our emotions and thoughts, it is impossible to develop coherent ethical views by accepting them as the authority on what we should do. We need some general guidance by which to decide which thoughts should have priority, or even whether they should be ignored altogether – for example, the first lecturer referred to his general ideas on fairness before following his immediate impulse to accept the late essay.

The moment-to-moment approach could not be adopted by members of professions, since they would have no acknowledged principles or values as the basis of their ethics. Nor would they be able to engage in the ethical reasoning and debate that is appropriate – and sometimes necessary – in professional contexts.

Professionals should not act on the basis of their emotions, any more than they should act on the basis of their personal values, without checking whether they comply with professional principles and values. They should not, for example, treat people differently simply because they have different emotional reactions to them.

Members of professions do not have professionally relevant reasons for treating people differently solely on the basis of their emotional responses to them. If it is right for professionals to treat people in a particular way in certain circumstances they should treat everyone in those circumstances in that way, irrespective of their emotional responses to them.

In this chapter we have seen that convictions about particular situations can have a part to play in professional decision making. However, we have also seen that professionals must refer to principles and not rely on developing ethical guidance solely from convictions. Nor should they act in accordance with their emotions and thoughts of the moment without reference to ethical principles.

In the next chapter we consider ways in which professionals can deal with dilemmas.

Questions

1. Is there a framework of ethical principles or anything similar that members of your profession are expected to pay heed to?

2. Are they expected to use their own judgement about how to apply any general guidelines to particular circumstances?

3. As far as you are aware, are the issues considered in this chapter ever discussed within your profession? If not, do you think it would be beneficial if they were?

4. Are there any legal or professional requirements on members of your profession that are relevant to the issues in this chapter?

Notes

1   While cultural values and perspectives do not form part of the criteria on which the committee's decisions are based, information about the cultural values and perspectives of people affected by their decisions may form part of the data the committee takes into account. Before deciding what ought to be done in a particular situation the committee must consider how its decisions are likely to affect people with particular cultural views, just as it must consider how they may affect people with particular disabilities, health conditions, and so on.

2   Tim Dare, in the *Encyclopedia of Applied Ethics* (1998, p.188), states that, '[Principles] are used to clarify, to diagnose, to structure discussion. They allow us to approach moral problems from as comprehensive a position as we can manage... They are tools in moral reasoning rather than self-contained machines for the generation of moral answers. *Moral deliberation should be conceived of not as a matter of simply applying decision procedures consisting of easy-to-follow rules, but as a matter of approaching particular cases in the light of general and perhaps competing theories and principles,* of previous relevant deliberations, and of appropriate knowledge of particular cases.' (The italics are mine.)

3   Those who take this case-study approach see all ethical thinking as starting from convictions about what it is right to do in a particular situation. However, it is questionable whether someone's conviction about a particular situation really is the beginning of their ethical thinking. As discussed in Chapter 3, no one can live in a value-free vacuum (i.e. without being aware of having been influenced by general ideas in their community as to the sorts of behaviour that are regarded as better or worse than others). So whether people are conscious of it or not, their convictions about particular situations are likely to be influenced by the general values of the cultural context in which they live.

Chapter 10

Dealing with Dilemmas

What is a dilemma?

People refer loosely to any situation in which they find it difficult to make a decision as a 'dilemma'. They may say they are 'in a dilemma' when they do not know what to do because they are uncertain about the facts of a situation. Strictly speaking, however, a dilemma is a situation in which people feel caught between 'right against right'. Expressing this in terms of principles, we can say that people experience a dilemma when they consider that:

- two or more ethical principles are relevant to their situation
- the principles make conflicting demands upon them.

Plato's man who promised to return an axe to someone who has since become a homicidal maniac experiences a dilemma. He sees two principles as relevant – keeping promises and preventing harm – but which should he follow?

Seeing dilemmas as irresolvable

There are various ways of responding to dilemmas, and in this chapter we consider which are appropriate in professional contexts.

Some people regard dilemmas as irresolvable because they think all ethical principles are absolute – that is, that all ethical principles should always be carried out. Consequently when they see two or more principles as making conflicting demands upon them they are stuck. If they meet the demands of one they will fail to carry out their duty to meet the demands of the other, and that is ethically unacceptable. On their view if the man returns the axe he acts immorally because he does not carry out his absolute duty to do what he can to prevent harm. If he does not return the axe he also acts immorally because he fails in his absolute duty to keep a promise. So there is no ethically acceptable solution. According to this view all the truly sensitive person can do is agonise over the irresolvability. The misery of people who think in this way is richly portrayed in novels, plays and opera, where it is often seen as the mark of a noble soul to be trapped in the agony of a dilemma.

There is, however, a practical and professional reason why this view should not be taken by members of professions. When ethical demands compete in a professional situation it is part of their job to use their expertise and skills – often in conjunction with clients – to work out a way forward. They cannot just wring their hands in agony: they have an obligation to do something.

There are also conceptual and ethical reasons for challenging the view that dilemmas require people to carry out two or more conflicting but absolute duties. To grasp the conceptual reason, consider what we would think of people who required others to do what is impossible. We would consider that they were treating the others unfairly. After further thought we might also consider they were conceptually confused, since if you know something is impossible you cannot meaningfully require someone to do it. Similarly, people who think that they are themselves ethically required to do what is impossible – namely, to fulfil the demands of two or more conflicting absolute principles – are conceptually confused. It is a conceptual error to think that ethics can make unfair or impossible demands upon us. We cannot have an ethical obligation to do what is impossible.

For practical, professional, conceptual and ethical reasons, then, members of professions should reject the notion that dilemmas require them to perform two or more incompatible and absolute duties, all of which are absolute. When faced with situations they see as dilemmas they must try to find ways forward.

Ways of addressing dilemmas

There are various ways of addressing dilemmas. Sometimes more than one is called for.

Interpreting principles

The first way of addressing dilemmas is to consider how the relevant principles should be interpreted in the particular situation. Since principles are general they allow for flexibility in their interpretation. Sometimes it is ethically appropriate to interpret and apply them to situations in ways that make them more compatible with each other than they at first appear. We saw an example of this in Tim's situation in the last chapter. Feeling caught between the demands to be truthful and to prevent harm, Tim considered his obligation to be truthful in that particular situation did not require him to tell the children all he knew about their parentage, so long as he did not lie to them.

Using their knowledge of situations to decide how principles should be interpreted and applied is part of the judgement professionals are expected to make. However, such decisions may not always resolve conflicts; hence, in addition to, or instead of, this way of addressing dilemmas, professionals may need to consider others.

Seeking a compromise

A second way of dealing with ethical demands that conflict in a particular situation is to seek a compromise between them. This involves looking for a course of action that goes as far as it can towards meeting the demands of all the principles, even though it may not be fully in accord with any one of them. Again, this approach requires careful consideration of the details of the situation. In the following case, for ease of illustrating the ethical issues, it is assumed that legal or professional requirements do not prescribe what the medical team should do.

> Max, a 35-year-old from outside the United Kingdom, is on a six-month assignment in London. He attends a hospital as he is suffering from severe and persistent diarrhoea and weight loss. The doctors suspect he may be HIV positive and ask to test him. Max agrees but only on the condition that the results are not divulged to anyone else. He is confirmed as positive.
>
> In subsequent discussion it emerges that Max is a firefighter. He has a wife and three children, aged seven, five and three, and has had sexual contact with other women since being in London. He does not want his wife to know about his condition as he fears it would end his marriage, nor does he want his employers to know as it may damage his career. He refuses to give the names of his sexual contacts.

Members of the healthcare team disagree about what to do. Some say their prime duty is to prevent future ill-health as much as possible. His wife should be told so that she and the children can be tested and treated if necessary. Some think his employers should be informed as there could be a risk of his infecting others, were he to be injured. Others, however, say they must abide by the agreement made with Max when he agreed to be tested and also respect his wishes. Staff see the conflict as between preventing further harm on the one hand, and keeping their promise and respecting Max's wishes on the other: a clash between obligations to results, integrity and autonomy.

At first it seems there is no way forward that will be acceptable to all the staff. It is then suggested that Max should be counselled to make him aware of the dangers to his family and colleagues, of the treatments that could be given to his family, if they are infected, and of the preventative measures that could be taken if they are not. The hope would be that once he appreciates the advantages of informing his wife he will agree to this initially and then, perhaps, to informing his employers.

This suggestion is influenced by all three ethical concerns but is not completely in accord with any of them. It keeps the promise but tries to get it annulled, it respects the patient's wishes but tries to change them, and it works towards the prevention of harm to others but does not take the immediate action that might be the best way of doing so. As such it is a compromise all the team can accept. Of course the counselling may not achieve its aim and Max may not change his mind. What should the team do then?

At this present stage the team does not have to make that decision, and, indeed, it cannot do so until that point is reached. For by then other factors may have become relevant. For example, if Max is to receive the medication he needs when he goes home, it may become clear to him that this is impossible without his wife learning of his condition, and this may partially resolve the situation. Moreover, the medical staff, who at present consider the promise should be kept and Max's wishes respected, may regard his views as irresponsible if he still refuses to inform his wife once he is aware of all the likely consequences of his condition. Or another course of action may then be suggested: for example, discontinuing Max's treatment until he gives permission to inform his wife. By such an action no promise would be broken and it might be an effective way of getting him to change his mind, thereby enabling further harm to be prevented. On the other hand, if he did not change his mind, withdrawing treatment would clearly not be in his interest – and many in the team might see working for this as their most important obligation.

In this example the team seeks a way forward that takes account of as many ethical principles as possible. The process is one of seeking a way forward that the people involved consider meets as many of their obligations as they can. Professionals cannot be required to do more than this. As we noted earlier, people do not have an ethical obligation to do the impossible.

Professionals should not underestimate the possibility of finding compromises between conflicting demands. People often, for example, regard the obligation to seek the best consequences as irreconcilable with the obligations to treat people fairly, and assume that they can only meet one obligation by neglecting the other completely. But actual situations sometimes provide scope for giving attention to each. We saw an example of this in the last chapter, where the health authority committee at first thought it must choose between going for the best long-term results and its obligations to current patients. However, it then found a way of doing something for each.

Giving priority to principles according to circumstances

When it is not possible to find a way forward by interpreting the principles in the ethical framework or by finding a compromise between them, a decision must be made to give priority to one, or to some, over the others.

The approach adopted in this book[1] is to regard all the principles as initially having the same level of importance, but to then give priority to whichever is considered the most important in the particular circumstances. Another way of putting this is to say that all the principles should be regarded as *prima facie* – that is, as principles that should be carried out unless the obligation to do so is overridden by what is considered to be a greater ethical obligation in the circumstances.

This approach gives professionals – whether working individually or in a team – the freedom to take account of whatever factors in a situation they consider ethically relevant, such as clients' interests, wishes and expectations, legislation, technical matters, likely consequences of various options, professional objectives, and so on, and the freedom to judge the relative importance of their ethical obligations in the light of all these. In some situations they may see the demands of one principle as more important than those of others, but in other situations they may consider their priorities should be reversed. For instance, the doctor with the army officer patient thought that in some circumstances he should give priority to keeping his promise over preventing harm, and in others that he should give priority to preventing harm. This flexible approach is familiar to most professionals. In some situations they may consider that they are justified in not telling people the whole truth to avoid them becoming unnecessarily worried, whereas in others they must tell them everything, even though it will worry them.

When deciding how to prioritise ethical obligations professionals should consider various questions. For example, in these circumstances:

- would preventing harm or bringing benefits to others necessitate failing to respect clients' autonomy

- would preventing harm or bringing benefit to others necessitate failing to pursue clients' interests

- how great is the harm to others likely to be if we respect clients' autonomy

- how great is the harm to others likely to be if we pursue the client's best interests

- how great is the likely damage to clients by not pursuing their interests

- how great is the betrayal of the client's trust in professional integrity and fairness by not pursuing his or her interests

- how great is the harm likely to be to this professional relationship and to the trust in professions generally by not pursuing clients' interests

- to what extent does not pursuing a client's interests undermine his/her autonomy and wishes

- is the obligation to pursue clients' interests more important in this situation than the obligation to prevent harm or to benefit others

- is the obligation to respect clients' autonomy more important in this situation than the obligation to prevent harm or to benefit others?

Such questions can be answered, and the relative importance of the answers judged, only after careful consideration of the particular circumstances of a situation.

As pointed out in Chapter 8, professionals should:

- not adhere to any principle only if they genuinely consider that, in a particular situation, its demands are ethically outweighed by the demands of the others or by any legal or profession-specific requirements

- be satisfied that what they do is the *only* way to meet these other demands

- do what they can to minimise their infringement of principles.

Despite the flexibility of this approach, regarding all principles as prima facie is not an 'anything goes' approach. If professionals in a particular situation decide to give priority to one principle over another, they should still comply with the other principles as far as possible. Let us return to the example of the health authority committee. If its members had decided to allocate its resources to educational and preventative health programmes, thereby giving priority to pursuing the best long-term results, it should still allocate the resources as fairly as possible. It should, for example, try to ensure that the programmes are available to all people who might benefit from them, whatever their cultural membership – that is, it should 'treat everyone alike unless relevant differences between them justify treating them differently'.

Seeing ethical principles as initially having the same level of importance in this way is, of course, compatible with professional advisory bodies drawing up guidelines on how professionals might normally prioritise principles in various types of circumstance. Guidelines might, for instance, suggest that when professionals are deciding their most general policies they should give priority to seeking the long-term best results and the welfare of people in general, but once these policies are being carried out they should give priority to the interests of the individual taking the programmes. For example:

> When academics are deciding what educational programmes to offer they should consider how they can contribute to the well-being of people generally by the provision of higher education, but when they are operating the programmes they should give priority to the interests of the students taking them.

The more professions are able to support their members by providing guidelines the better, though individuals should still have the moral responsibility of deciding *how* the guidelines should be applied to their particular situation.

Ethically appraising a situation

The following suggestion for how professionals should approach a situation puts together points from this and previous chapters.

1. Prior to thinking of ethical aspects, ascertain whether there are any legal or professional requirements that prescribe what should be done. If there is none, or if requirements allow some freedom of action, ethically appraise the situation as follows.

2. Consider which of the four ethical principles are relevant to the situation.

3. Note the ways in which any professional guidelines or accepted rules of thumb, or you as an individual, normally interpret and apply these principles in relation to your professional task.

4. Consider whether these interpretations and applications should be varied in relation to your particular situation.

5. If the demands of the principles conflict when related in the way you think appropriate to your task and situation, consider:

    ◦ whether there is an acceptable compromise that meets as many of the demands as possible

    ◦ if not, what is the relative importance of the demands in the situation.

6. Consider how you can minimise any infringement of any principles.

7. Act accordingly.

For an example of this approach we return to the doctor worrying over whether or not to tell the army about his patient's condition.

1. For the purposes of this example only, we assume there are no legal requirements that prescribe what the doctor should do, and that any relevant professional guidelines give him some freedom of choice.

2. The doctor sees three principles as relevant to his situation: to seek best results, to respect autonomy and to act with integrity.

3. He and/or professional guidelines normally see(s) the demands of these principles as:

    ◦ to seek the best results for all affected by the situation

    ◦ to respect the wishes of an informed and competent patient

    ◦ to abide by the explicit or implicit promise of confidentiality and to work for the best interests of the patient.

4. When deciding whether to tell the army, he applies the principles to his particular situation as follows.

    ◦ With regard to seeking the best results, he thinks the probability of harm to army personnel, if the army is not informed, is such that it outweighs the likely harm to the patient of telling them. He therefore sees his consequential obligation as to tell the army.

    ◦ With regard to autonomy, he sees no reason to change his normal interpretation of this: he still thinks he has an obligation to respect his patient's informed wishes.

    ◦ With regard to integrity, again he sees no reason to change his normal interpretation of his obligation both to confidentiality and to work for the patient's interests.

5. He considers that the demands of seeking the best results conflict with respecting the patient's autonomy and with keeping confidentiality. He is uncertain, however, as to what would be in the patient's interests. He cannot see any compromise between the ethical demands, and decides he should give priority to preventing the likely harm to many people.

6. When thinking how he might infringe his obligations both to autonomy and confidentiality as little as possible, the following thoughts occur to him:

    ◦ To tell the army no more than that the patient's condition is such that his judgement might be adversely affected by stress.

○ To do what he can to ensure the army treats whatever information he gives it on a confidential, strictly need-to-know basis.

○ In future, to improve the integrity of his working practices by making clear to patients at the outset that there are situations in which, as well as his obligation of confidentiality to them, he may have an obligation to divulge information to others.

You may think that there are other ways forward in the doctor's situation that he fails to consider.

Regret and blame

Even when professionals ethically appraise their situation as conscientiously as they can, and even when they find a course of action they think satisfies as many ethical demands as possible, they may still find it difficult to reconcile themselves to what they do. They may feel badly about not being able to fulfil all the ethical demands they see in the situation, even though they accept it is impossible to do so. As Beauchamp and Childress put it (1989, p.5):

> If a prima facie duty is outweighed or overridden, it does not simply disappear or evaporate. It leaves what Robert Nozick calls 'moral traces'.[2] The agent should approach such a decision conscientiously and should expect to experience regret and perhaps even remorse at having to override and infringe this prima facie duty.

When the doctor decided he should tell his patient's employers about his condition he may well have felt regret at not respecting his autonomy and breaking confidentiality, even though he is convinced it is the right course of action to take. When people have such misgivings they should not confuse them with feelings of guilt. If they have done the best they can to meet as many ethical demands as possible, they cannot be held – by themselves or others – guilty for not doing more. They should at most regret not being able to meet more demands. Despite what Beauchamp and Childress say, people in such a situation should not feel remorse, since remorse is a feeling of sadness at having acted unethically or immorally. They have not acted unethically, even though they have not met all the ethical demands they perceived in the situation. So they should not blame themselves. Nor should they blame others in a similar situation. As long as people have carried out their ethical appraisal as best they can, they cannot be held morally blame-worthy.

We look briefly at blame in the next chapter.

Questions

1. What sort of situations in your profession present members with dilemmas?

2. If members find a dilemma intractable, is it accepted practice that they discuss it with colleagues, either formally or informally?

3. Do you think such a practice may be beneficial?

4. Could there be problems with such a practice?

5. Are there any legal or professional requirements on members of your profession that are relevant to the issues in this chapter?

Notes

1 There are two other ways in which the four professional ethical principles might be prioritised. We consider each briefly here and say why neither is appropriate for professionals.

 1. *Putting principles into a fixed order:* If principles are put into a fixed order then the first principle always takes precedence over the second and the second over the third, and so on.

 The obvious problem in arranging the four ethical principles in a fixed order is that this restricts professionals' flexibility. For example:

 ° if respecting autonomy were given precedence over seeking the best results, professionals would always have to respect the autonomy of everyone they could, no matter what disastrous consequences were likely to follow

 ° if seeking the best results were given precedence over autonomy, professionals would always have to seek the best results, however marginally they were the best, and however much pursuing them went against the informed decisions of the individuals most involved in the situation.

 2. *Regarding 'seeking the best results' as the absolute principle, and giving the other principles varying importance:* This way of prioritising principles reflects a traditional view in ethical thinking that what ultimately matters are the consequences of what we do, and so seeking the best results should be

our only ethical concern. On this basis professionals would regard this as the absolute principle, and would give differing importance to the rest only if they might promote the best results in particular circumstances. On the other hand, if complying with any of the other principles would be likely to prevent the best results, they should be ignored.

If professionals were to adopt this view, when there was no clash between pursuing the best interests and their other obligations, they would still have their other obligations. But whenever they thought that treating people fairly, or respecting their autonomy, or acting with integrity, could have an adverse effect on results, they would have to give priority to results. They could not consider a compromise between pursuing results and their other obligations, since a compromise would not carry out the pursuit as far as possible, and so would be highly likely to have an adverse effect on the results. Consequently, all professionals all of the time would see their most important obligation as to produce the best results over the long term. Whenever they were convinced that a particular course of action would do this, they would have to carry it out regardless of how much it would treat people unfairly, fail to respect people's autonomy or damage their own professional integrity.

On the other hand, if professionals do not see the consequential principle as absolute, but on the same level of importance as the other principles, in every situation they must consider whether pursuit of the best results would infringe their other obligations. If they think it would, they must consider whether the likely increase in value of the results justifies infringing them. Moreover, as part of their professional accountability, they must be prepared to explain why they thought they were justified in not carrying out their other obligations. But if they regard the consequential principle as absolute, they need not give attention to any of this.

A further issue would arise if professionals were to regard seeking the best results as absolute. If they were to make this known to the population, as they should if they are to act with integrity, or if the population were to realise that this was how they worked, it would adversely affect people's trust in them. If people thought professionals would not treat them fairly, respect their views, or act with integrity towards them, if better results might be obtained by not doing so, their confidence would be shaken. And if professionals were to try to hide the fact that they always regarded seeking the best results as their priority, by doing so they would, in effect, abandon the other ethical principles.

When people seek the services of professionals, they want them both to pursue valued objectives and to act fairly, with integrity and respect their autonomy. And when these values conflict, people want to be able to trust professionals to make a careful and balanced judgement as to how best to deal with the situation. Whatever the professionals decide – whether in conjunction with their clients or not – people want them to be accountable for their decision, and to be able to say why, in those particular circumstances, they thought it right to do what they did. People want to see that in their deliberations professionals gave serious consideration both to their obligation to seek the best consequences and to their other obligations to the individuals who use their services.

2   Nozick, R. (1968) 'Moral Complications and Moral Structures.' *Natural Law Forum* *13*, 1–50.

Chapter 11

Blame

To be blamed is to be judged to be at fault. In this chapter we are considering whether people should be judged to be *morally* at fault, not whether they are *legally* at fault. People get obsessed with blame: they blame themselves and they blame others. It is a sad fact that many organisations become interested in ethics because they are more concerned with blame – how to escape it and how to apportion it – than with ensuring that ethical considerations inform their activities. Yet (as we shall see) the conditions that have to be met for someone to be fully blameworthy do not often occur. Indeed some psychiatrists and psychotherapists consider they never do. They claim that when we understand what makes people behave as they do, we see they have little, or no, choice and so do not deserve to be blamed.

In this book (as discussed in Chapter 3) we take the everyday view that most people much of the time have a degree of choice, and that members of professions often have the opportunity to consider what they ought to do and the freedom to do it. We have argued that when these opportunities occur professionals have a moral responsibility to decide what they ought to do by taking into account the four professional ethical principles and any guidelines specific to their profession. The message of this brief chapter is that professionals are not morally blameworthy so long as they carry out this responsibility to the best of their ability.

In many organisations there is a tendency to blame people whenever they do something that has unfortunate consequences, even though they may not be blameworthy. Unwarranted attribution of blame has the following damaging effects.

- Individuals become afraid to act in ways they consider both professionally appropriate and ethically justified, in case their actions have unforeseen consequences for which they are then blamed.

- If a disaster occurs, and debriefing procedures take place to find out what happened, colleagues close ranks and disclose as little as possible in order to avoid blame being attributed to the individuals who make decisions and take action. As a result organisations fail to 'learn from their mistakes'.

- The lives of many professionals are ruined by guilt and blame, whether attributed by others or by themselves.

In this chapter we consider when blame should and should not be attributed, in the hope that a better understanding of the issues will mitigate these harmful effects.

Clearly, a very brief chapter like this can do no more than indicate some of the main considerations professionals should bear in mind when concerned with issues of blame. Those whose work involves making judgements about the responsibilities of colleagues, or who take part in disciplinary proceedings, debriefing procedures and similar activities, should consider the issues in far more detail than can be dealt with here.

When are people morally blameworthy?

People are, in basic terms, blameworthy for what they do only when they are both causally and morally responsible for it. People are causally responsible for something when they cause it to happen. They are morally responsible for something when:

- they have some choice over what they do
- they are aware of the likely implications of what they do, or are at fault for not being aware of them; such implications for professionals include the likely effects of their actions and whether, by their actions, they will treat others unfairly, fail to respect their autonomy, or lack integrity.

If a man pushes a woman down a steep flight of stairs then he is *causally* responsible for her fall. Whether he is also *morally* responsible depends upon:

- whether he pushed her deliberately or it was an accident
- whether he was, or should have been, aware of the likely effects of his behaviour.

If we discover that he knocked into her because he was rushing, and we think he should have been aware of the dangers of doing so at the top of a busy staircase, then to that extent we may consider he was morally responsible – and blameworthy. However, if we later find out he was rushing to reach an injured person, we might reduce the extent to which we hold him blameworthy because we think he was under pressure to rush and had a good reason to do so.

From this the following points emerge:

- From the fact that someone causes a disaster it does not necessarily follow that he or she deserves any blame.

- There can be degrees of blame; someone may be only partially morally responsible for what they do.

The point that people deserve to be blamed for something only to the degree that they are morally responsible for it is obscured by the fact that we often 'blame' *things* – rather than people – merely because they cause something to happen. If there is a poor attendance at an outdoor gathering people may 'blame' the rain; by this they mean that the rain caused people to stay away. They do not mean that the weather could have, and should have, done something else, or that it is morally responsible (and blameworthy) for not doing so. On the other hand, if they blame the publicity manager for the poor attendance, they probably do mean that, on their understanding of the situation, he could have, and should have, been more active, and so is blameworthy.

Let us consider another example:

A doctor gives her patient less treatment than she would be expected to give someone in his condition because she has inadequate resources.

If lack of resources is not the result of any failure on the doctor's part, she cannot be blamed for it or for the way she treats her patient. Even though her patient may have been treated unfairly, she should not be held morally responsible for this as she had no choice. She may feel regret at not being able to treat the patient more fully, but she should not feel remorse, since she has not acted immorally.

In such a case it may be difficult to know whether anyone is morally responsible for the lack of resources or for the unfair treatment of the patient: is it the management team that did not allocate enough resources to the doctor, the governmental department that did not allocate enough resources to the management team, or the people who elected the government into office? It may be that no one can be regarded as morally responsible and blameworthy. This example brings home the points that:

- the people who are causally responsible for the unethical treatment of someone may not be the people who are morally responsible for it

- others, or no one, may be morally responsible.

Let us look at a slightly different situation:

A doctor has limited resources – for which she is neither causally nor morally responsible – for a particular form of treatment. After carrying out an ethical appraisal of the situation as fully and carefully as she can, she decides to use the resources she has for one patient rather than another, because the treatment would be likely to increase the life expectancy of the one patient far longer than the other.

Given the lack of resources, the doctor has very limited choice over what she does, and so only to that limited extent has she any moral responsibility for the way she treats her patients. However, since she exercises her limited choice in a way that fulfils her ethical obligation – she appraises the situation as carefully as she can and makes a decision based on ethical criteria – she cannot be blamed for not giving the treatment to one of the patients.

Whether individuals deserve any blame for what they do, and how much they deserve, can be decided only once there is full understanding of their situation, including their knowledge, intentions and powers, and the degree to which they have considered their ethical obligations.

From these considerations we see that it is unjust to blame people (including ourselves):

- if they have no choice over what they do and no responsibility for the situation in which they find themselves, *or*

- if they have some choice and when exercising it they fulfil their ethical obligations to the best of their ability.

What does 'fulfilling their ethical obligations to the best of their ability' entail for professionals?

Professionals generally fulfil their ethical obligations when:

- they are as well informed and equipped as they can be, given the time, resources and facilities at their disposal – this includes

  ◦ being up to date with relevant professional expertise

  ◦ knowing details of the case in hand

  ◦ trying to anticipate situations that may arise, and being prepared for them as much as possible

  ◦ developing working practices that allow time for preparation

- they consider all ethical principles, and any ethical guidelines and legal requirements relevant to the situation, and apply them as they think fit, so that

  ◦ they genuinely think that the balance of ethical demands upon them is such that they should act as they do (see Chapter 10, p.170)

  ◦ if asked, they can fully account for their decision to act as they do.

These conditions give a responsibility to professions and organisations to ensure that:

- systems are in place to inform and prepare personnel as fully as possible

- personnel know the importance of incorporating ethical and legal considerations into their working practices and, if appropriate, are trained to do so.

Questions for a debriefing process

People conducting a debriefing process should consider stating at the outset that its main purpose is to discover why working practices failed to avoid problems, rather than to apportion blame. During the process they might raise questions similar to the following, the aim of which is to avoid misattribution of blame, while enabling the process to be an effective way of learning from past mistakes.

1. What were the factors and actions that caused the problems, and why did they occur?

2. To what extent were the actions of identifiable persons causally responsible for the disaster?

3. Did those individuals have adequate expertise, information, facilities and time to do their job properly?

4. If not:

   (a) were these inadequacies caused by failures in the organisation

   (b) what can be done to ensure they do not occur again

   (c) were the inadequacies caused by shortcomings in the working practices of the personnel involved

   (d) what can be done to ensure they do not occur again?

5. Were harmful consequences and unacceptable treatment of people caused, partially or wholly, because personnel did not consider the ethical and legal aspects of their work?

6. (a) Had personnel been adequately informed and trained to make these considerations?

   (b) If not, what can be done to ensure that any inadequacy does not occur in the future?

7. (a) Did personnel have time to reflect?

   (b) If not, what can be done to ensure they have time in the future?

8. In view of their awareness of the ethical and legal issues and their time to reflect before acting, could personnel be reasonably expected to have anticipated the unfortunate consequences, and to have taken steps to avoid them?

9. If personnel took the actions they did for ethical and/or legal reasons, can they give an account as to why they thought their action was appropriate?

10. (a) If they can give an account, does it show they reflected as carefully as can be expected in the circumstances?

    (b) If not, what can be done to ensure personnel give more careful reflection in the future?

11. (a) If personnel reflected on ethical considerations, was their line of thought reasonable?

     (b) If their line of thought is considered unreasonable, what can be done to ensure it is not followed by others in the future?

12. (a) In the light of answers to the previous questions, did personnel have the freedom to act differently from how they did?

     (b) If not, what can be done to ensure personnel are not put in this situation again?

13. (a) In the light of answers to the previous questions, to what extent, if any, should personnel be regarded as morally responsible for what happened?

     (b) To what extent is it just to blame any personnel for what happened?

     (c) If it is just to blame them, what benefits and/or harm are likely to follow from doing so?

14. What further lessons can be learned from this debriefing process for the future (e.g. can the conduct of debriefings be improved over the way this one has been carried out)?

Questions

1. Do you know how debriefing procedures work in your profession?

2. Are there any legal or professional requirements on members of your profession that are relevant to the issues in this chapter?

Chapter 12

Rights

Chapter 3 states that the principle to respect moral rights is omitted from the professional ethical framework because the moral rights professionals should respect can be derived from the principles included. This chapter explains this point further, after providing a guide to rights.

Different sorts of rights

Claims about rights – for instance, 'John has a right to freedom of speech' – imply that people have rights as a matter of fact, rather as it is a matter of fact that someone has brown hair. This is because claims about rights have the form (or 'surface grammar') of descriptions: 'Jane has a right to abortion on demand' and 'Jane has brown hair' have the same grammatical structure.

Consequently the claim that Jane has the right to abortion on demand seems like a description of Jane. It seems to be stating a fact about her. It may, however, be expressing a moral opinion. It may be saying that the speaker thinks the services for an abortion ought to be available to Jane. Whether it is making a claim about facts or expressing an opinion depends upon what sort of 'right' the claim is about.

If it is about legal, social or institutional rights it is a claim as to what the facts are – for example, the speaker may be claiming that, as a matter of fact, Jane has a legal right to abortion on demand. On the other hand, if the claim is about natural, human or moral rights it is expressing an opinion – the speaker is saying he thinks Jane should be able to have a pregnancy terminated if she requests it.

We therefore need to know what sort of rights people are talking about before we can know whether they are making a claim about facts or expressing an opinion. Let us review the different sorts of rights.

Legal rights

Legal rights are bestowed upon individuals by the law of a state. Whether someone possesses a legal right to do something (e.g. to walk across a piece of land) or to be protected from something (e.g. the legal right not to be treated by a doctor without giving consent) is a matter of fact, which can be ascertained by referring to the law of that particular state.

Social rights

Social rights are rights that develop by custom and practice within a society or community – for example, the right for people to be served in a shop in the order in which they join a queue. Whether or not it is a fact that such a right exists can be ascertained by observing what normally happens within that community, and what expectations people have within it.

Institutional and professional rights

These are rights granted by the rules of an institution, club, association or profession, such as the right to use a library or the right to call oneself a chartered physiotherapist. Whether or not it is a fact that someone has such a right can be ascertained by referring to the formal rules of the organisation or the profession to which that person claims to belong.

Natural rights

Natural rights are rights that people claim to exist because of what they think is 'natural'. This is a version of the view that nature is a guide as to how we ought to live, which we looked at in Chapter 1. As we saw in that chapter, people have different notions of what is 'natural', depending on their beliefs, their social customs and the particular aspects of nature they select. John Locke, for instance, living in England in the seventeenth century, claimed that all people are *by nature* equal, and so have a natural right to individual freedom (Locke 1988). Others, however, claim that it is natural for humans to live in societies in which some people control others.

Because people's views as to what is 'natural' vary, they disagree as to what rights are 'natural'. Moreover, as we saw in Chapter 1, it is often not possible to arbitrate between their claims by carrying out an objective observation of the facts of nature, since people disagree as to which facts should be considered and how they should be interpreted. Consequently, claims about natural rights are opinions, disguised as claims about natural facts. Because they are claims about what ought to be the case, they are moral claims, and so natural rights are a form of moral rights (see below).

Human rights

Claims about human rights assert that people should be treated in certain ways because they are human. They imply that it is a fact that all humans have certain rights. But is it?

Consider Article 25 of the United Nations Declaration of Human Rights, which states: 'Everyone has the right to a standard of living adequate for the health and wellbeing of himself and of his family...' This statement cannot be claiming it is a fact that all humans have either a legal, institutional or social right to an adequate standard of living, since not everyone in all societies does. Some states may give their citizens a legal right to one; some societies may have customs whereby all people are considered entitled to one; and some institutions may have rules that all their members should be provided with one. But by no means does everyone have a legal, social or institutional right to an adequate standard of living. Since Article 25 is not stating a fact, it is expressing the opinion that everyone ought to have an adequate standard of living. It is also usually understood as implying that governments or societies should try to provide an adequate standard for everyone. So, even though Article 25 has the form of a statement of fact, it is expressing a moral opinion – an opinion as to how people ought to be treated because they are human. It is, therefore, a type of moral right (see below). This is true about all assertions of human rights, unless they are about human rights that have been incorporated into legislation – they are then legal human rights.

Moral rights

Moral rights are claims about rights that express moral opinions. As we have seen, they may be based on views about nature or human nature, in which case they are known as natural rights and human rights.

Consider the following assertion: 'Women have just as much right to speak their mind as men.' If this assertion is intended to express the opinion that women's views should be expressed and listened to just as much as men's, it is claiming a moral right.

Some people are attracted to the view that ethics is based on moral rights because they are misled by the surface grammar of rights claims and see them as stating facts rather than as expressing opinions. Consequently rights-based ethical views seem to them to be unchallengeable. They think it is a fact that people have certain moral rights, including human and natural rights. So if others disagree with them, they think the others are denying the truth of these 'facts'. This can make them intolerant of the views of others. As a result, some human rights campaigners, for example, have the zeal found in fundamentalists of any persuasion: they consider they have a duty to impose what they see as the truth on everyone, since anyone who disagrees with them is living in factual error.

Reasons for professionals to think in terms of principles and obligations, rather than 'moral rights'

There is a close connection between obligations and rights, such that if people have obligations to others, then the others normally have rights to be beneficiaries of those obligations. If the obligations are legal ones, the corresponding rights are legal ones, and if the obligations are ethical ones, the corresponding rights are moral ones.

So if professionals have ethical obligations:

- to work for the interests of their clients, their clients have a moral right to have their interests promoted by professionals

- to treat people fairly, their clients have a moral right to be treated fairly and justly

- to respect clients' autonomy, their clients have a moral right to have their autonomy respected

- to act with integrity, their clients have a moral right to be treated honestly by professionals.

The relative strength of these moral rights in a particular situation depends on the perceived strength of the ethical obligations in that situation. Consequently, if people see a conflict between moral rights, to attempt a resolution they should consider which of the corresponding ethical obligations in the situation are thought more important, or whether a compromise between them can be found.

For example, if someone claims that a patient's husband has the moral right to know her prognosis, but someone else claims the patient has a moral right to confidentiality, the relative importance of these rights can be discussed by considering:

- the consequences of telling and not telling the husband and, from this, the relative importance of seeking the best results
- the relative importance of the professional's obligation to respecting the patient's autonomy
- the relative importance of keeping any promise to the patient
- whether the integrity of the health team will be compromised by telling the husband if they have promised confidentiality, and the relative importance of their integrity.

We can now see why, in the professional ethical framework of principles, there is no reference to respecting moral rights. This is because the moral rights relevant to the work of professionals correspond to obligations derived from the principles that are already included. Consequently, by adopting the four principles in the framework, professionals subscribe to the values underlying any moral rights they should take into account. For example:

- claims that everyone has a moral right to education or to the protection of the law can be derived from views that
  - the greatest benefit over harm is likely to be achieved if everyone has access to these services
  - it is unfair that some people should not have access to these services
  - it is unjust for benefits not to be made available to individuals according to their needs (in these cases their needs for healthcare, education and protection from others)
- claims that someone has the moral right to be told the truth – say about their health and its prognosis – may be derived from the obligations of professionals
  - to act with integrity by being truthful
  - to enable patients to make informed, autonomous decisions
- claims that professionals have a moral right to certain resources may be justified by pointing out that their integrity is undermined if they cannot provide the services they are expected to offer at an appropriate standard, or that there are likely to be damaging consequences if they try to operate without them.

If people discuss their opposing moral views in terms of ethical obligations and principles, rather than by making assertions and counter-assertions about moral rights, they are more likely to understand the reasons for each other's views. From this understanding they may come to respect each other's opinions, or even to find a way forward that is mutually acceptable. But if their exchanges remain at the level of contradictory claims about rights, this is unlikely to happen.

Understanding rights claims

Although moral rights are not included in their ethical framework, professionals need to be aware of the general nature of rights claims, since people make them all the time. The following points apply to all forms of rights.

- Rights – whether legal, social, institutional or moral (including natural and human) – may be positive or negative.

- Positive rights are rights *to* something (e.g. rights to healthcare and education). Moreover, if people say someone has a positive right (e.g. to education) this normally implies that there is a duty or obligation on the part of others (e.g. the state, parents or a profession) to provide for it.

- Negative rights are rights *from* something, such as the right not to be tortured or not to be treated by a doctor without giving consent. Negative rights impose restrictions on others.

- Rights serve the interests of individuals. Positive rights do so by giving them things, such as opportunities. Negative rights do so by protecting them from things, such as interference from others.

- To claim that an individual has a particular right has implications for how others should treat that individual. For example, someone who tells a doctor that her patient 'has a right to a bit of peace and quiet now' implies 'I think you should do less – or no more – invasive treatment'.

- If people have rights, others have responsibilities and obligations towards them. For example, if employees have legal rights, employers have legal duties and responsibilities towards them.

- Possessors of rights may also have responsibilities and duties – one of which is to decide when to exercise their rights.

Here are some examples to illustrate the last point:

> A child protection officer may have the legal right to take a child away from its parents, but it does not follow that she should always exercise that right. It is her responsibility to decide when it is appropriate to do so.
>
> Similarly, if I think you have the moral right to express your opinions, it does not follow that I think you should express them on every occasion. Instead I think you have a responsibility to decide when to do so. So, if a friend invites you to his house, which he is very pleased with, I may think it wrong of you to tell him that you think it is a ghastly place. However, since I think you have the right to express your opinion, if you decide to tell your friend your views, then I do not think I am entitled to prevent you from doing so. On another occasion, of course, I may think you have a duty to express your opinion. If you are a member of a multi-professional care team attending a meeting to discuss policy in relation to individual clients, then I may think you ought to state what you think from the perspective of your particular expertise.

From these considerations we see that to claim people have rights implies that the possessors of rights and others have responsibilities and duties in relation to those rights.

Questions to ask about rights claims

When a claim is made that X has a right to Y, to be clear what is being said, professionals may find it useful to ask the following questions.

1. Is this a claim that X has:

    - a legal right

    - a social right

    - an institutional or professional right

    - a natural, human or other type of moral right (see the following paragraph)?

    It may sometimes be unclear which type of the above rights is being claimed. If someone says, 'Everyone has a right to freedom of speech', they could be saying that they think this is a legal right or that they think it is a moral right. When

someone talks about human rights it may be unclear whether
they are talking about legal human rights (i.e. human rights
that have been incorporated into legislation) or whether they
are talking about human rights that have not been
incorporated.

2. What is the basis for the rights claim?

If the claim is about a legal, social, institutional or
professional right, the truth of the claim can be checked by
finding out whether the law of the land, the customs of the
community, or the rules of the institution or profession
actually give X the right that is being claimed.

   If what is being claimed is a moral right, human right or
natural right, you need to know what ethical concerns (or
which beliefs about what is 'natural' to humans) lead the
speaker to make the claim.

3. If the claim is of a moral, human or natural right, what sort of
demand is the claim making?

Claims of moral – including human and natural – rights
sometimes express the opinion that people ought to be given
certain legal, social or institutional rights. Sometimes they
simply express the opinion that others ought to treat them in
certain ways. For example, 'All women have a right to
abortion on demand' could be expressing the *moral* view that
women should have the *legal* right to have an abortion
whenever they request one, or it could be expressing the view
that healthcare professionals should always agree to women's
requests for an abortion.

We will now use these questions to clarify what is being claimed by the first
Article of the UN Declaration of Human Rights.

   Article 1 states, 'All human beings are born free and equal in dignity and
rights. They are endowed with reason and conscience and should act
towards one another in a spirit of brotherhood.'

1. What sort of right is being claimed here?

All humans are clearly not born into societies in which they
are all equally free, all regarded as of equal dignity, and in

which they all have the same legal and social rights. Consequently Article 1 cannot be making a claim that all people actually have equal legal, institutional or conventional rights.

Moreover, the claim is not factually true in saying that all humans are born with reason and conscience. Some people, unfortunately, are incapable of reason, and it can be argued – as do many psychologists – that no one is born with a conscience but that a conscience is something people develop if they are in an appropriate social environment.

So Article 1 is not a factual description of what is actually true, but a moral view – it is about what ought to be true.

2. What is the basis for the rights claim?

Since all the articles in the UN Declaration refer to 'Everyone' or 'No one', and state that each right applies to all human beings, it is clear that part of the justification for the Declaration as a whole is, in fact, the principle of justice as fairness. The Declaration demands that in so far as we are all alike in being human, it is just and fair that we should all be given the same rights. Indeed, to describe something as a human right involves making this ethical point.

3. What sort of demand is the claim making?

The speaker (in this case the United Nations) seems to be expressing the opinion that all human beings ought to live under legal and social systems that:

- give everyone the same legal and social protection
- give everyone the same freedoms and rights
- value everyone equally.

Question

1. Are there any legal or professional requirements on members of your profession that are relevant to the issues in this chapter?

Postscript

The aim of this book has been to encourage members of professions to reflect on the values they espouse in their practice. If they agree with the views put forward, the book will give them confidence in values that are appropriate for their work in culturally complex democratic societies and can help them treat people of different cultures fairly.

These values can form a simple but supportive framework of principles (summed up by the mnemonic 'FAIR') to help professionals make the balanced judgements so often necessary, whether they are working as individuals or as members of professional and advisory bodies.

- **F***airness*
- **A***utonomy*
- **I***ntegrity*
- **R***esults* ™

Readers interested in applying the ideas in this book to their own professional situation are invited to visit: www.richardrowson.org.

References

Beauchamp, T.L. and Childress, J.F. (1989) *Principles of Biomedical Ethics*, 3rd edn. New York: Oxford University Press.

Bentham, J. (1843) Volume II of *The Works of Jeremy Bentham*. Edited by J. Bowring. Edinburgh: William Tait.

Brunner, E. (1947) *The Divine Imperative: A Study in Christian Ethics*. London: Lutterworth.

Dare, T. (1998) 'Applied Ethics, challenges to' in *Encyclopedia of Applied Ethics, Vol. 1*. London: Academic Press.

Department of Health (2002) *UK Code of Conduct for National Health Service Managers*. London: Department of Health.

Facione, P.A., Attig, T. and Scherer, D. (1978) *Values and Society: An Introduction to Ethics and Social Philosophy*. Englewood Cliffs, NJ: Prentice Hall.

Gilby, T. (ed. and trans.) (1951) *St Thomas Aquinas: Philosophical Texts*. New York: Oxford University Press.

Hare, R.M. (1981) *Moral Thinking: Its Level, Method and Point*. Oxford: Oxford University Press.

Locke, J. (1988) *Two Treatises of Government*. Edited by P. Laslett. Cambridge: Cambridge University Press. (Originally published in 1689.)

Mill, J.S. (1960) *Utilitarianism, Liberty and Representative Government*. London: J.M. Dent and Sons.

Mill, J.S. (1974) *On Liberty*. Edited by G. Himmelfarb. London: Penguin. (Originally written in 1860.)

Rawls, J. (1971) *A Theory of Justice*. Cambridge, MA: Harvard University Press.

United Nations (1948) *Universal Declaration of Human Rights*. www.un.org/Overview/rights.html

Further Reading

The following list aims to give an indication of the variety of books available that deal with issues raised in *Working Ethics*.

General expositions of ethical thinking

Benn, P. (1998) *Ethics*. London: UCL Press.

Bentham, J. (2001) *The Collected Works of Jeremy Bentham*. Oxford: Clarendon Press.

Hospers, J. (1996) *Human Conduct*. Fort Worth: Harcourt Brace.

Mill, J.S. (2004) *Utilitarianism*. Belle Fourche, SD: R.A. Kessinger Publishing.

Rachels, J. (2002) *The Elements of Moral Philosophy*. New York: McGraw-Hill.

Thompson, M. (2005) *Ethical Theory*. London: Hodder Murray.

Ethics and the professions

Bok, S. (1986) *Secrets*. Oxford: Oxford University Press.

Chadwick, R. (ed.) (1994) *Ethics and the Professions*. Aldershot: Ashgate.

Chadwick, R. (ed.) (1998) *Encyclopedia of Applied Ethics, Vols I–IV*. San Diego: Academic Press.

Corey, G., Corey, M. and Callanan, P. (1984) *Issues and Ethics in the Helping Professions*. Florence, KY: Brooks Cole.

Davis, M. (2002) *Profession, Code and Ethics: Towards a Morally Useful Theory of Today's Professions*. Aldershot: Ashgate.

Davis, M. and Stark, A. (eds) (2001) *Conflict of Interest in the Professions*. New York: Oxford University Press.

Kleinig, J. (1986) *The Ethics of Policing*. New York: Cambridge University Press.

Koehn, D. (1994) *The Ground of Professional Ethics*. London: Routledge.

Oliver, P. (2003) *The Student's Guide to Research Ethics*. Maidenhead: Open University Press.

Villiers, P. (1997) *Better Police Ethics*. London: Kogan Page.

Index

Page numbers followed by 'n' refer to note entries.